Making Room for Change

Making Room for Change

Finding Ways to Leverage Time to Benefit All Students

Amanda Bastoni, Brian Pickering, and Nathan Bisson

ROWMAN & LITTLEFIELD

Lanham • Boulder • New York • London

Published by Rowman & Littlefield
An imprint of The Rowman & Littlefield Publishing Group, Inc.
4501 Forbes Boulevard, Suite 200, Lanham, Maryland 20706
www.rowman.com

Copyright © 2021 by Amanda, Bastoni, Brian Pickering, and Nathan Bisson

All rights reserved. No part of this book may be reproduced in any form or by any electronic or mechanical means, including information storage and retrieval systems, without written permission from the publisher, except by a reviewer who may quote passages in a review.

British Library Cataloguing in Publication Information Available

Library of Congress Cataloging-in-Publication Data

Names: Bastoni, Amanda, 1980- author. | Pickering, Brian, 1965- author. | Bisson, Nathan, 1992- author.
Title: Making room for change : finding ways to leverage time to benefit all students / Amanda Bastoni, Brian Pickering, Nathan Bisson.
Description: Lanham : Rowman & Littlefield, [2021] | Includes bibliographical references. | Summary: "This book provides practical knowledge and examples of an evolving scheduling system known as the Flex Time Model. The philosophical shift to this model allows educators to be more creative with how to present and effectively implement their curriculum"—Provided by publisher.
Identifiers: LCCN 2021009186 (print) | LCCN 2021009187 (ebook) | ISBN 9781475847185 (cloth) | ISBN 9781475847192 (paperback) | ISBN 9781475847208 (epub)
Subjects: LCSH: School day—United States. | Flextime—United States. | Effective teaching—United States.
Classification: LCC LB3033 .B38 2021 (print) | LCC LB3033 (ebook) | DDC 371.2/42—dc23
LC record available at https://lccn.loc.gov/2021009186
LC ebook record available at https://lccn.loc.gov/2021009187

Our book is dedicated to the many committed teachers across the country who have given their professional lives to their students. Through continuous changes, pressures, and budget constraints, teachers have stayed the course with one constant, to help students grow and learn. Our sincere thanks to our three spouses, all teachers. Thank you Abe, Kerry, and Allegra for all you do for students and your families!

Contents

Foreword		xi
Preface		xiii
Introduction		1
	Questions to Ask	2
	Why Is Change Needed?	3
	Bailey's Story	6
	Questions to Ask	9
1	Step 1: Make a Philosophical Shift—Implementation	11
	Create a Vision, Not a Set of Rules	11
	SDT: Autonomy, Competence, Relatedness	12
	Autonomy	14
	Competence	19
	Relatedness	23
	Jessica's Story	28
	Bill Leahy's Perspective	33
	School Culture: The Key to Success and How Flex Time Helps It Improve!	35
2	Step 2: Understand the Structure—Implementation	39
	The Flex Time Model in Practice	41
	Flex Time Scheduling That Fits	43
	Timing and Mentor Groups	44

Types of Flex Time Learning Opportunities	44
What Is and What Is Not Flex Time?	45
Using Flex Time Data to Drive Instruction and Supports	51
How to Collect Flex Time Data and Use It to Improve Student Success	52
The Value of Time: A Teacher's Perspective	53
Flex Time: College and Career Readiness	55
Marena's Story	58
Flex Time: How to Change the Concept of "Homework" to "Practice"	60
Flex Time Scheduling Software	64
Note	71

3 Step 3: Making it Real—Implementation — 73

Steps to Success for Implementation	73
Schuyler's Story	78
Lily's Story	80
Successful Implementation of Flex Time in Your School	84
How to Create Flex Time Protocols	88
Flex Time: Setting Up an Advisory/Mentor Group	90
How to Support Self-determination through the Flex Time Model	95
Autonomy	95
How to Support Autonomy through the Flex Time Model	97
Competence	98
Relatedness	100
How to Support Relatedness through the Flex Time Model	103
Response to Intervention and the Flex Time Model	104
How to Support Response to Intervention through the Use of Flex Time	106
How Flex Time Benefits Extended Learning Opportunities	106
Background on Seat Time vs. Flex Time	107
How Flex Time Helps Make School/Business Partnerships Possible	109
Impact of Flex Time on Student Success and Its Value to the Business Community	110
Impact of Flex Time and Extended Learning Opportunities in the School	111
Time Provided for Extended Learning Opportunity Teachers	112

	Conclusion	114
	Final Considerations	114
4	Flex Time Model Checklists	121
	Flex Time Model Protocols	124
	Say Flex Time Survey Questions	125
	General School Questions	125
	Teacher Questions	125
	Student Questions	126
	Parent Questions	126
	Interest Level Flex Time Survey for Teachers	127
	School-Based Flex Time Survey Annual Questions	128
	General School Questions	128
	Teacher Questions	128
	Student Questions	129

References   131

About the Authors   137

Foreword

They say time is a precious commodity. For schools, it is perhaps the most important resource available, yet it often serves as a scapegoat for why educators are unable to provide students with the individual support needed for success. We have all heard the excuses: "Our schedule prevents us from doing that," "We don't have the time to meet," or "There aren't enough hours in the day to get it done."

It's time to put an end to this. Effective schools are finding ways to leverage time to work for *all* students and *all* educators committed to a vision of learning for all, whatever it takes. This new approach breaks from traditional beliefs long held about how time is used in schools.

For over a century, schools in the United States have used time, specifically "seat time," as the standard measure of learning. The practice was developed at the turn of the Twentieth century by the American industrialist and steel mogul, Andrew Carnegie, to bring about a level of standardization the U.S. education system had never seen before. Since then, the "Carnegie Unit," defined as 120 hours of contact time with an instructor, has been the widely accepted way to award academic credit and quantify student achievement. The practice is based on this assumption: if students are provided an equal amount of time, then they can master a predetermined amount of material.

In the past 20 years, educators have challenged this approach, suggesting there are more effective ways to measure student learning without using time as the constant. Their efforts have given rise to the personalized learning movement—one that calls for a shift from a system that measures learning by the minutes a student sits in front of a teacher to one based on mastery of learning objectives. This movement goes by different names in different parts of the country, such as competency, proficiency, mastery, or standards-based learning. These models have come to challenge the organizational structure in today's schools in the United States. If schools are to no longer use seat time to measure student learning, how will that impact how time is used?

Carnegie's vision led to the modern-day schedules that exist in schools today. These schedules allow schools to set predetermined amounts of time to be spent on various learning activities. Schedules in most schools have become quite complicated over the years as more and more time has been designated for various nonacademic programming. Year to year, every iteration to a school's schedule is designed to try to make for a better match to students' needs. The problem is these schedules often lack opportunity for both personalization and flexibility.

Now more than ever, schools need to operate with schedules that allow maximum flexibility of time to meet students' needs. There is increased demand for individualized and personalized time for reteaching, intervention, and enrichment. Educators need time for collaboration on matters related to curriculum and lesson planning and for calibration of their instruction, assessment, and grading practices. Students need flexibility to use time in different ways, too—and flexible scheduling promotes greater student agency and equity for all.

It is time we stop thinking of time as a fixed constant we need to work around but rather a variable we can leverage to meet the individual needs of each and every one of our students. This book by Bastoni, Bisson, and Pickering will challenge your thinking on how to use time in this way. It might just be the game changer your school has been looking for.

Brian M. Stack—NH high school principal (Sanborn Regional High School), Solution Tree author, competency-based learning specialist, 2017 New Hampshire secondary school Principal of the Year.

Preface

This book on flex time came to be because of the clear and obvious tool that we all discovered in a short amount of time while building this model. With all of the many changes in education that we have endured, none tied everything together for students and teachers more than flex time. Each contributing author and writer to this book worked with flex time in a different role, but each shared the same enthusiasm for the impact it was having on student culture and performance.

As we completed this book, we entered into the COVID-19 pandemic. We believe the one positive to this sudden challenge in our world is the realization that flex time can be effective in our schools. The focus moving forward should be on learning outcomes, experiential learning, interventions, and extensions. It is our belief that we should move away from the traditional "seat time" for credits theory which seems more obvious than ever.

This has been true of all roles in education at a time where having a positive impact on our young people is more critical than ever. It is our hope and strong belief that implementing a system of flex time will not only improve learning for students but also take pressure away from our teachers outside of their school day. Teachers will be able to access students as needed during the day and not have to rely on the "hit or miss" of after-school help sessions.

Teachers are the heart and soul of our educational systems and will always play a valuable role. We hope that this tool allows current and aspiring teachers the opportunity to prepare their own strategies to successfully help their students.

Introduction

Many educational reforms are based on a management consultant approach, which relies on a visiting expert to create large-scale, systemwide, and, oftentimes, cookie-cutter solutions. In many cases, this approach does not take into account particular circumstances or needs of a given school, and typically changes do not last.

The flex time model is not this kind of reform.

It does not require an expert to implement. The flex time model is designed to be *flexible*. It is designed to be *user friendly*. It is designed to support *personalized learning*.

What the flex time model requires most to be successful is a philosophical shift—a commitment to a school based on ideals rather than rules.

The flex time model starts by restructuring the school's current learning environment so there is a flexible chunk of time every day where students can engage in a variety of activities, such as relearning missed or misunderstood information, making up tests, participating in enrichment projects, earning additional credits, reteaching competencies, working on college applications, or even getting counseling for social/emotional purposes.

At one school, flex time may be 35 minutes, while it could be 50 at another school. According to Pickering (2015), a former high school principal in New Hampshire (NH) and the creator of the flex time model, this new reform makes room for schools to implement the changes they need. The block creates a space in the school day to do homework and to improve grades, behavior, and student engagement. After implementing the flex time model,

90% of students at Pickering's high school agreed flex time offered them opportunities to improve their learning. These high school students not only experienced significant positive changes following the first full year of flex time implementation but also had a 31% decline in D and F grades.

The process of implementing the flex time model typically starts by making small reductions in class, lunch, and passing times and then allocating these reductions to create a new block during the school day. Flex time can be used for a variety of purposes—that is the beauty of the model. Some schools, for instance, place flex time at the end of the day, and some schools place it in the middle of the day. Some schools use flex time to provide additional homework time, some schools schedule club meetings during flex time, and still others offer enrichment activities, such as jazz band or school newspaper club.

Since Pickering created the flex time model, other school leaders, such as Brian Stack, a high school principal in Kingston, NH, and the 2017 New Hampshire Principal of the Year, have adopted and praised the model. Stack (2017) credited the flex time model with an increased ability to personalize learning at his high school. Andrew Brauch, a former high school assistant principal in New Hampshire said, "After the first semester of implementation, I saw a 25% increase in As, and a 44% increase in Bs" (Pickering & Bastoni, 2016, p. 11). Guy Donnelly, a high school principal in Wolfeboro, NH, said, after implementing the flex time model in 2013, he saw a "dramatic increase in student attendance" (Pickering & Bastoni, 2016, p. 10).

The flex time model does not rely on the latest professional development seminar, workbook, or high-stakes tests. There are no books to buy or curriculum to implement. The flex time model requires a shift in philosophy and implementation of a structure that opens up space in the schedule for *creativity*. The flex time model becomes a vision—a vision that makes room for change.

QUESTIONS TO ASK

When considering whether the flex time model is a good fit for your school, ask yourself the following questions: does my school have . . .

- a schedule where students share the responsibility to improve their own learning?

- a schedule where students have time to complete their school work during the school day?
- a schedule that relies primarily on after school time to get the help they need?
- a schedule where students can get timely extra help when struggles are first recognized?
- a schedule where students have time to participate in enrichment opportunities during the school day?
- a schedule where teachers have time during the school day to help all students succeed?
- a schedule where school counselors could provide group or individual support sessions without disrupting students and teachers during their regularly scheduled courses?

WHY IS CHANGE NEEDED?

The bell rings, and class begins. A lesson is taught, students engage in learning, and then, regardless of what is happening—even if a student has just asked a particularly insightful question—the next bell rings, and class is over. For the average high school student in the United States, this pattern continues for 6–7 hours a day, 179 days a year, over the course of 4 years.

Throughout the school day, students are told when to start learning and when to stop, given standardized tests at predetermined points, and told when and where they can eat. They must ask for permission to go to the bathroom, and, if they are found in the hallway without a pass, they are punished. Despite the educational push to embed 21st-century skills into schools (e.g., critical thinking, innovation, problem solving, creativity, and self-direction), students learning in the current educational structure are given very few opportunities to practice autonomous thinking or make choices about how they spend their time in school. This structure is the de facto environment for learning in the United States. This is school.

In their book, *Most Likely to Succeed*, Wagner and Dintersmith (2015) call this approach the "assembly-line model of education" (p. 25). According to the authors, this school structure "excelled at what it was designed to do: train millions of young adults to perform repetitive tasks quickly, retain modest amounts of content, and keep errors to a minimum" (Wagner & Dintersmith,

2015, p. 25). Wagner and Dintersmith (2015) are critical of this approach, as is the educational reformer Ken Robinson, who argues the current structure, which is based on the needs of the Industrial Revolution, decreases motivation for learning and creativity (Robinson & Aronica, 2015).

Robinson refers to the modern school structure as a "culture of compliance" where deep learning and questioning is "actively discouraged, even resented" (Robinson & Aronica, 2015, p. X). Another educational reformer and the creator of the Programme for International Student Assessment, Schleicher (2018), believes the current school structure is problematic because it focuses on "standardization and compliance" (para. 9) and not on skills needed to be successful in adult life, such as collaboration, emotional intelligence, original thinking, innovation, or a sense of responsibility to others and the world. Jack (2018) believes students "need fewer facts and more skills to apply knowledge in novel situations: a move from memorization to elaboration" (p. 1).

The current school structure provides students with little control and stems from a behaviorist approach in which external motivators, such as rewards and punishments, are used to mandate compliance. This structure provides "little room for either free will or complicated processes such as memory, reflection, emotional reaction, and relational negotiation" (Toshalis & Nakkula, 2012, p. 8). Behaviorist approaches to teaching focus on creating learning environments in which behavior is modified through threats, arbitrary deadlines, pressured evaluations, and imposed goals. This approach can leave many students struggling to succeed.

This approach creates a serious problem. As educational thinker Alfie Kohn (2010) wrote, "Students who have almost nothing to say about what happens in class are more likely to act out, tune out, burn out, or simply drop out" (p. 4). Students who feel disengaged may express this feeling through aggressive behavior, defiance, and power struggles. In a meta-analysis of 800 studies, homework and smaller class size had less of an impact on student learning than a "lack of disruptive students in the classroom" (Hattie, 2009, p. 33).

In the 1980s, *A Nation at Risk* warned a "rising tide of mediocrity in [the] education system threatened the nation's security" (National Commission on Excellence in Education, 1983, para. 1). This report became a catalyst spurring educators to look for ways to redesign schools and increase the quality of learning environments (Newmann & Wehlage, 1995). Many researchers believed, by restructuring classroom environments, they could engage students in more relevant learning, which could, in turn, result in deeper understanding and ultimately higher scores, even on standardized assessments.

So, why is the demand for educational reform still being made today? Because simply reforming schools is not enough. Not all reforms work. In fact, many so-called reforms still glorify standardization and develop a narrow range of skills instead of supporting the development of skills that the reformer claims are essential for today's world. According to Zhao (2009) and Robinson and Aronica (2015), school reforms should focus on developing grit, confidence, and collaboration. Schools should push for a "more balanced and individualized and creative" (Robinson & Aronica, 2015, p. xvii) approach to education. In 2015, co-authors Robinson and Aronica shared their concerns about the current educational structure:

> One of my deepest concerns is that while education systems around the world are being reformed, many of these reforms are being driven by political and commercial interests that misunderstand how real people learn and how great schools actually work. As a result, they are damaging the prospects of countless young people. (p. xv)

The flex time model fits in a strand of reform called the Effective Schools Movement. Since the 1960s, the focus of this reform method was to determine best practices for education of all children. Supporters of the Effective Schools Movement sought to understand ways to create an "educational setting in which children make the progress necessary to prepare them for the next level of learning" (Horn, 2010, p. 335). While numerous researchers have added to and informed this movement, the self-determination theory (SDT) in particular has provided guidance on elements necessary to create educational environments that impact learning for all (Hunt et al., 2010).

Deci and Ryan (1985), key researchers in SDT, have found that humans have a natural tendency to act in effective and healthy ways; however, outside forces, such as social or cultural factors, can support or inhibit these natural motivations, which, in turn, impact overall well-being and performance. SDT outlines three psychological needs that, when met, lead to an increase in positive intrinsically motivated behaviors and affect overall satisfaction and well-being. These needs are competence, autonomy, and relatedness. SDT asserts learning environments with these characteristics are less likely to be filled with students who are disruptive, resistant, and/or disengaged—and more likely to have students who can persist with learning, even if they are not doing well academically.

On the other hand, when students perceive their environment is controlling, or when they lack feelings of competence, relatedness, and autonomy, they are more likely to engage in power struggles with those in authority, and they are at a higher risk of dropping out (Hardre & Reeve, 2003). Taken on the whole, research on SDT reveals a cycle of lack of motivation when students learn in environments they perceive to be controlling, cold, or overly difficult. Students who perceive they have little autonomy, relatedness, or competence are more likely to disengage from learning; students who disengage from learning are more likely to be expelled or suspended; and students who are suspended or expelled are more likely to drop out of school or perform poorly academically (Hattie, 2009; Wauchope, 2009).

The current school structure originated more than 100 years ago. It was designed to teach students basic skills, compliance, and routine task completion. The structure was based on a behaviorist philosophy of education, which relied on external motivators in a controlling environment. The current structure holds standardization of student knowledge as the final goal (Rose & Ogas, 2018) and rewards compliance.

Students learning in these types of environments feel a lack of autonomy, relatedness, and competence and are more likely to become disengaged from learning. They are also at a higher risk for dropping out of school. The flex time model is a new school structure spreading quickly across the United States. Anecdotal and qualitative evidence reveals that this model increases student success by creating learning environments where students feel more of what they lack in the traditional learning environment: autonomy, relatedness, and competence.

BAILEY'S STORY

As a paraprofessional, coach, teacher, athletic director, assistant principal, and principal in education over three decades, conflict sometimes occurred with a student's ability to access the staff member they needed during the school day. The common practice was for students to meet with teachers for extra support after normal school hours, but that was ultimately not timely and came with frustrations from students, teachers, club advisors, and coaches because of time missed from one activity or another.

At his high school one morning in the fall of 2010, Brian Pickering was standing outside greeting students. One of his students, Bailey, was walking into school and stopped to see him, hoping he could assist her in getting some teacher assistance that day. The conversation went something like this:

Bailey: "I need to get help today from my physics teacher. Could I get a pass to go see her during advisory?"
Brian: "Bailey, I wish I could let you go there during advisory, but if I let you leave advisory to get help from your physics teacher, then I would have to allow every student to have that same opportunity. I can't do that, but could you go see her after school?"
Bailey: "Mr. Pickering, I play field hockey, and the playoffs are coming up. I can't miss today's practice."
Brian: "Right. I don't want you to miss practice either. I completely understand that. How about during lunch?"
Bailey: "Mr. Pickering . . . lunch is only 23 minutes, plus my physics teacher doesn't have the same lunch as I do."

Bailey went on with her school day, and Brian's mind was spinning as he thought, "I can't help a student get extra help from her teacher in physics?" Specifically, his frustration was with the inability to have a student access a teacher in a timely manner to support her academic needs for the day. This student was not wasting time in class, and she was not skipping classes—she was simply a driven student who was busy and wanted assistance to be successful.

Brian decided, in that moment, if a student needs help from a specific teacher, they should be able to see them and in a timely fashion, not with a "hit or miss" approach that relies on teacher and student availability. He could not imagine being in the business of educating all students where they have to rely on luck to get the extra help they need. For over a century, he felt they had relied on this hit-or-miss system of timely support for their secondary students.

Brian brought the problem to the staff. Together they created a team of people who recognized the same ongoing concern in secondary education and who were willing to commit to a process that would solve this problem for their school. They were solving the problem for their school, but what the team may not have realized then was, just a few years later, their work and a new technology solution would pave the way for thousands of students across the country to make a valuable change to the flex time model.

This dedicated team, including teachers from each discipline, counselors, and an administrator, began building an educational model driven by the following essential question: *how can we fit Response to Intervention (RTI), relearning, mentoring, advising, enrichments, extensions, and social/emotional supports effectively into the school day?*

This interdisciplinary team wanted to build something that included perspectives from all of the various roles in education and not another directive from a principal or the administration in general. These teachers wanted to build a flex time model that allowed the time and space for all students and staff to work together collaboratively. Teachers wanted and needed time to work together and the freedom to experiment, and, as an administrative team, we knew this was important for the school to become successful.

During the original implementation of the flex time model, students would start their week on Monday in their advisory room. Instead of staying in that room for the entire week, like in the former advisory model, flex time gave students the ability to move to the teachers and spaces where they could get the support and tools they needed in a timely manner. If they were passing classes with higher than a D, they could schedule time with any teacher from whom they needed or wanted help during that week. This was the basic start of flex time. Every student could finally get help from their specific teachers who could directly support them on their assignments and their growth as effectively as possible. This seems like a commonsense approach, but it has been missing in our secondary schools across the nation.

Traditional study halls have provided students with time during the day but without the structure to allow students the opportunity to seek the academic support they need from the specific teacher who can provide it. Have you ever sat in a cafeteria or auditorium where a staff member is monitoring study hall? Students are frequently sleeping, and when Brian was in high school, he loved to see how many times he could fling a pencil and get it to stick in the ceiling above. The goal for students and the staff monitor is to simply get through the time in study hall, which rarely includes direct interaction between students and individuals who can provide academic support. There is no better source than getting help and individualized attention from a teacher.

Bailey's situation was not unique, as many students struggled with time. Brian witnessed this as a teacher when students said they did not have time to complete their homework and as a coach when a student-athlete had to miss important practices to meet with a teacher after school. As an administrator, there were many students who sat in detention for failing only because they did not get their homework done. All of these scenarios continued to happen in a cookie-cutter educational system that did not allow for student autonomy or access to a flexible educational model.

QUESTIONS TO ASK

In this section, we learned more about the history of the current school structure in the United States. We also heard about the kinds of barriers this structure can create for students like Bailey. Before implementing the flex time model, we want to make sure you understand the barriers at your school by answering the following questions:

- What supports are in place at my school to ensure students like Bailey can get the help they need? (Make a list.)
- What barriers might prevent a student from accessing these supports? (Make a list.)
- Have you ever been in a situation with a student like Bailey? Has a student or parent ever reached out to ask for help or support and it was difficult to find the time?

Chapter 1

Step 1: Make a Philosophical Shift—Implementation

Motivation, performance, and development will be maximized within social contexts that provide people the opportunity to satisfy their basic psychological needs for competence, relatedness, and autonomy.

(Deci et al., 1991, pp. 327–328)

CREATE A VISION, NOT A SET OF RULES

The most important attribute any school can have is a positive school culture. Research has shown direct connections between positive school cultures and increases in students' self-esteem, learning, academic success, personal growth, graduation rates, reduced school violence, enjoyment of school, internal motivation for learning, and success later in life. But creating a positive school culture is incredibly complicated. Teachers need to feel excited about coming to work, students need to feel empowered to learn, and parents and community members need to be engaged. In other words, to achieve a positive school culture, staff, coaches, visitors, and everyone in the school community need to feel valued and cared about.

That's a lot of work!

Creating a positive school culture is not something that can be addressed by a quick fix or an "out-of-the-box" solution. It is a bigger job than any one person can do alone. It takes a team. It also takes space. Just like a garden, keeping a positive culture producing positive results and successful outcomes for students year after year requires ample room for growth. The flex time model creates that room, because it creates a learning environment where there is room for choice, relationship building, and personalized learning.

SDT: AUTONOMY, COMPETENCE, RELATEDNESS

The flex time model is theoretically based on self-determination theory or SDT. For this reason, to successfully use the flex time model, schools and school leaders must first embrace the philosophical belief that all stakeholders will do better when they work and learn in conditions that support autonomy, competence, and relatedness. SDT makes it clear that environments that meet the need for student autonomy will be motivating, while environments based on rewards, deadlines, pressured evaluations, or imposed goals will diminish motivation (Ryan et al., 2013). Learning environments where students report feelings of autonomy, competence, and relatedness have been linked to higher grades and increases in concentration and persistence (Ryan et al., 2013).

Further, SDT researchers have shown that when students are educated in environments that support autonomy, competence, and/or relatedness, they demonstrate better conceptual learning (Grolnick & Ryan, 1987), more creativity (Koestner et al., 1984), and a more positive affect toward both regular (Ryan & Grolnick, 1986) and special educational settings (Deci et al., 1992). SDT provides a framework for looking at elements in a learning environment and serves as a "basis for predicting which social contextual factors will promote versus forestall students' involvement in learning and effective adjustment to the complex social world" (Deci et al., 1996, p. 172).

SDT can be used as a lens for understanding environments that are the most conducive to learning and student success (Deci et al., 1991), because schools can control and influence characteristics outlined in SDT. For example, according to Malian and Nevin (2002), "Self-determination can be seen as an ecological phenomenon that emerges as the individual interacts with the environment and as the environment shapes new responses on the part of the individual. Therefore, the process of self-determination is teachable" (p. 74).

Learning environments that support student needs, as outlined in SDT, have also been associated with greater student interest, less pressure and tension, greater persistence, higher self-esteem, more trust, and better psychological and physical health (Ryan & Deci, 2013). In a study on intrinsic motivation, Cordova and Lepper (1996) found, when facilitators used autonomy-supportive techniques, such as contextualization, personalization, and choice, students showed a "dramatic" increase in motivation and depth of engagement in learning. In their study, published in the *International Journal of Innovation and Scientific Research*, Akram et al. (2014) found a strong positive correlation between perceived autonomy and student achievement.

Educational researchers agree psychological health improves problem-solving and thinking skills (Robertson, 2010), and "psychological well-being is a necessary foundation for optimal cognitive functioning, learning, and engagement" (p. 5). For these reasons, and because characteristics outlined in SDT can be directly impacted by the school environment, successful school reforms should include development of learning environments that meet students' needs.

SDT was developed from the tradition of humanistic psychology, specifically the concept of "human potential" (Deci et al., 2013). Humanistic potential theories assert that people naturally move toward growth and development, and, given the right circumstances, all people inherently strive for self-actualization or full potential (Deci et al., 2013). SDT provides a deeper understanding of what ingredients are needed for humans to reach full potential or full functioning (Deci et al., 2013). According to SDT, social-environmental factors, specifically feelings of autonomy, competence, and relatedness, dramatically influence cognitive and behavioral patterns (Deci et al., 2013; Silva et al., 2014). When these three needs are met, individuals begin to engage in intrinsically motivated behaviors that can increase a positive sense of self and lead to healthy full functioning.

Students learning in conditions that develop feelings of autonomy, competence, and relatedness will be more engaged with their learning and more likely to be motivated (Deci et al., 1991), while students learning in conditions that do not support these needs will become "defensive, reactive, and compliant" (Deci et al., 1996, p. 172). Conversely, students learning in environments that do not support these needs and that are based on rewards, deadlines, pressured evaluations, or imposed goals will ultimately experience diminished levels of motivation (Ryan et al., 2013), which may cause students to disengage from learning. Disengagement and diminished levels of motivation are often linked to disciplinary activity, and disciplinary activity can be related to dropping out of school (State of New Hampshire Department of Safety, 2018).

SDT provides a framework for predicting variables in the learning environment that will have positive effects on students' abilities to reach full potential and increase success in learning (Deci et al., 1996), which will have harmful impacts. By increasing students' feelings of autonomy, competence, and relatedness, according to SDT, schools will notice a reduced dropout rate and maximized learning environment.

Autonomy

For this study, the terms *autonomy* and *self-advocacy* refer to self-determination skills that allow a student to set learning goals and take charge of their own learning. According to Daly-Cano et al. (1995), "Self-advocacy is the ability to communicate one's needs and wants and to make decisions about the supports needed to achieve them" (p. 213). Student autonomy is developed when students are provided with a sense of choice or control.

Research has shown, when students perceive that they are in an environment that supports autonomy, they will experience enhanced personal growth, an increase in enjoyment of academic work, increases in creative thinking, positive emotions in the classroom, deeper conceptual understanding of new concepts, and even an increase in success later in life (Deci & Ryan, 1987; Deci et al., 1991). Autonomy has also been found to increase the internal motivation of learning for all students, including those with special needs and those considered gifted. Deci et al. (1991) explained SDT this way: "Motivation, performance, and development will be maximized within social contexts that provide people the opportunity to satisfy their basic psychological needs for competence, relatedness, and autonomy" (pp. 327–328).

According to SDT, school is primarily a socializing influence on young people's lives and, in turn, helps to prepare them for participation in society. In environments where students are given control or autonomy, they can begin to construct personal identities, move toward self-actualization, and engage in goal-oriented, self-regulated behaviors (Deci et al., 1991)—all skills and practices that better prepare them for life after high school. For example, Malian and Nevin (2002) found students with disabilities who were given the opportunity to practice and develop SDT skills while in high school were more likely to be employed and earn more money per hour. Malian and Nevin (2002) stated that SDT "is a predictor of successful transition to adult life. Students with disabilities whose IEPs and ITPs include self-determination goals, objectives, and processes are more likely to be successful upon exiting their school programs" (p. 74).

In 1996, Cordova and Lepper found autonomy was a key factor that increases students' intrinsic motivation. In fact, autonomy not only increased motivation but also produced dramatic increases in student engagement in learning, how much they learned over a fixed time period, and their perceived competence. Cordova and Lepper (1996) explained, "Students who were offered a modicum of choice over instructionally incidental aspects of learning contexts showed greater increases in motivation and learning" (p. 726). Or, as Clarke (2013) wrote, "Volition drives [student] inquiry" (pp. 6-7).

One educational approach, universal design for learning (UDL), has formally documented the importance of autonomy by characterizing the concept of choice as one of the key strategies a teacher can use to ensure all students have an equal opportunity to learn. According to the National Center on Universal Design for Learning (2012), UDL principles are research-based guidelines and approaches to teaching that, when incorporated in the classroom, increases learning for all students. Increasing autonomy, according to UDL theory, is a teaching technique that results in increased learning for all students. The recommendations UDL offers are all based on multiple replicable findings and educational research.

Experimental and quantitative evidence, as well as research and expert opinions, has revealed providing students with choice and autonomy has a direct impact on students' behaviors, values, and academic achievements (Kohn, 1993; National Center on Universal Design for Learning, 2012). For example, Kohn (1993) found increasing students' feelings of autonomy can actually increase test scores. Autonomy is also a key factor in reducing student burnout, fostering creativity, and developing less aggressive and less controlling behaviors in individuals (Deci & Ryan, 1987; Kohn, 1993; Rubin, 2012). Based on UDL research, student autonomy can be enhanced and/or suppressed. In their study, Assor et al. (2002) found that autonomy-supportive behaviors include fostering relevance, allowing criticism, and providing choice; autonomy-suppressing behaviors include not allowing criticism, intruding, and forcing tasks that are not meaningful for students.

Students' feelings of autonomy can be impacted by parents, peers, school culture, or specific teaching practices (Daly-Cano et al., 2015). Reeve (2006) found teachers can be taught to increase the level of autonomy support they provide to students, and an autonomy-supportive teaching style will help engage students and develop better teacher-student relationships. When teachers use noncontrolling language, use students' preferences, help students understand why an assignment or project is useful, and are open to receiving negative feedback from students, they increase students' internal feelings of control. Teaching students how to seek help or self-advocate, and giving them opportunities to practice these skills, ultimately, leads to more success academically (Douglas, 2004; Malina, 2002).

In 2008, researchers from Stanford University and the University of Rome tracked 412 students from age twelve to twenty-two. Results showed students who experienced "less of a decline in self-regulatory efficacy" (Caprara et al., 2008, p. 528) or autonomy as they continued through school were more likely to get higher grades and less likely to drop out of school. The UCLA Center for Mental Health in Schools Program and Policy Analysis (2011) stated, "Numerous studies have shown opportunities to express preferences and make choices lead to greater motivation, academic gains, increases in productivity and on-task behavior, and decreases in aggressive behavior" (p. 5). Literature on self-determination also has shown autonomy-supportive environments contribute to academic success and the likelihood of students remaining in school (Caprara et al., 2008).

When considering how to restructure schools, policymakers and administrators must place a high priority on structures that increase opportunities to promote, teach, and practice self-advocacy and determination skills. Regardless of reforms, selected schools of the future must allow student choice over such areas as time management and goal setting, thus shifting responsibility for learning back into students' hands (Rubenstein, 2011). Kohn (1993) went so far as to say:

> The evidence to support that view is so compelling that it is frankly difficult to understand how anyone can talk about school reform without immediately addressing the question of how students can be given more say about what goes on in their classes. (p. 4)

Autonomy and the flex time model: in a qualitative research study on the flex time model, students in a high school using the flex time model chose words like "choice," "options," and "freedom" to describe their experiences (Bastoni, 2019). For example, one student said:

> I think some other schools don't give a lot of freedom to students. And, I think that has a detrimental effect on how they learn . . . I think being able to have choice really makes you feel less like you're being locked down into a chair for an hour. Then they cut the chain, then you can go to another one, chain down to the desk, until the day ends. . . . So even just giving a little bit of choice with [the FTM], I think that's a nice way to help break up the day, make it less monotonous.

During interviews, students associated having choice or control with positive feelings, and they routinely mentioned flex time as one of the only times during the school day they experienced these types of feelings. As a senior from the study said, "I don't know any other time during the day kids get to schedule themselves." A freshman added flex time provided "[customizability] so kids aren't just constantly hating school all the time . . . it makes school a little bit more free, you know?" Students reported they appreciated having the option to move around the school and having more control over how they spent their time once they arrived at a destination. Another senior said flex time had "a good impact" on the entire school because it gives students the choice to go where they want. Other students said they liked being able to go "anywhere" and participate in a variety of options from "ceramics to gym to woodshop."

"The coffee shop opens, so you can go get a drink and wake yourself up. There's just plenty of opportunities . . . but it's just the overall freedom of it that's pretty good," said one senior. A freshman echoed this sentiment, saying flex time gives students "the opportunity to have fun in open gym or signing up for something else you'd like to try. . . . It gives kids a lot of options." Another freshman student's observations were also similar: "I don't think kids like it when people tell us what we have to do—I think we should be able to pick what we want, if it's appropriate."

In addition to the observations and feelings of autonomy students described, adults believed the autonomy provided by the flex time model was key to students' success. "Kids get a chance to get help, to reassess, to do enrichment projects, to take control of their learning," said one teacher. Another teacher connected flex time and student autonomy:

You're either getting the help you want, you're hanging out in a teacher's classroom you like, you're being quiet and not bugging anyone, none of those are negatives. . . . As a kid, I would love it, because I'm not forced, really, to sit in this classroom. They're forced to sign up, more or less. They're forced to be somewhere, more or less. But it's not like, bell just rang, I have to go to my next class.

Another teacher described what she liked best about flex time and, in doing so, clearly made a connection between the flex time model and the SDT characteristic of autonomy:

The purpose of it is what I like about it, that the kids get to decide where they go and what they need. So, I mean, there are definitely times when I'm like, "Um, no, you're not going to go play board games today because you missed your last three math summatives, and your teacher came over and told me that." But, as a whole, the kids get to advocate for themselves and decide what their areas of need are and how they're going to meet them. So, certainly we offer some support as they go through that process, but it's really up to them.

Even administrators made connections between the learning environment created by the flex time model and the SDT characteristic of autonomy. For example, one administrator shared:

It basically sends a message to kids that we recognize your time is valuable and important, and our goal is to personalize things as much as possible. So, to that end, we give you the opportunity to personalize how you spend some of your time because, depending on your classes and the time of the year, you need more time or less time for certain things.

Questions on autonomy: autonomy is one of the key tenets of SDT, and an increase in autonomy is one of the major outcomes of the implementation of the flex time model. Therefore, it is important to understand the role autonomy already plays at your school, what the perceptions of autonomy are, and what some of the barriers might be. Spend some time thinking about and taking notes on the following questions:

- How would you describe autonomy to a parent? A teacher? A school board member? Why do you believe it is important? How would you sell it?

- Does your school value autonomy? Why or why not?
- What activities do students have control over at your school?
- What activities do teachers have control over?
- What are the barriers to increasing autonomy at your school?
- Can you think of stakeholders who would work with you to increase autonomy at your school?

Competence

SDT recognizes that, to be successful, people need environments that support autonomy and competence. The concept of competence does not relate to how well an individual performs a specific task, such as reading a paragraph or solving a math equation. Instead, SDT refers to competence as a general sense of navigating the world and moving toward success. In a study on competency and autonomy, Deci et al. (1992) found students with learning disabilities who had experienced high levels of failure in school had a strong correlation between their own feelings of competency and their success in certain subjects. Essentially, when students felt competent in a subject, they were more likely to persevere and ultimately had better educational outcomes.

In 1978, Vygotsky introduced the zone of proximal development (ZPD), which can be understood as the space between what a learner can do unaided and what they can accomplish with the help of someone more experienced. Vygotsky argued educational challenges need to be presented slightly ahead of the learners' actual ability, but support must be provided to avoid discouragement, which can result in disengagement. Scaffolding is a term used in education to describe this approach and the supports given to help students move through that space.

To create environments where students feel competence does not mean creating environments that are not challenging. Instead, teachers who employ the concepts of ZPD and scaffolding acknowledge learning happens when students move from what they know toward what they want to know, but in a specific and supported way. In this same way, these educators rely on the belief that students who do not feel competency in a subject or in a classroom will need more support, but, as they continue to learn, they will develop stronger and stronger feelings of competence and need less assistance.

The flow theory of learning (Shernoff et al., 2003) sheds light on the connection between feelings of competence and learning as well. Flow is a state of mind characterized by deep personal enjoyment associated with a challenging activity perceived as slightly greater than the individual's ability. Similar to the ZPD, students who are experiencing flow may not be experts at the activity and are still experiencing the activity as a challenge; however, they feel competent enough to engage in the task (Shernoff et al., 2003). Students who experienced flow in the classroom were much more likely to be engaged and much more likely to learn (Shernoff et al., 2003).

When students were engaged, they experienced increased feelings of flow because they perceived they had control over what or how they were learning, and because they viewed themselves as being capable of participating. According to Shernoff et al. (2003), "Teachers may be able to enhance engagement by supporting students' sense of competence and autonomy, such as providing tasks that offer choice, are connected to students' personal goals, and offer opportunities for success" (p. 172). In other words, flow is directly related to the characteristics of competence and autonomy, as highlighted in SDT.

In 2003, researchers from the University of Iowa asked if self-determination, as a motivational model, could explain rural students' likelihood to persist or drop out of high school (Hardre & Reeve, 2003). The researchers found the "provision of autonomy support within the classrooms predicted students' self-determined motivation and perceived competence" (Hardre & Reeve, 2003, p. 347) and, in turn, predicted students' intentions to drop out of school. Essentially, students are more likely to persist at tasks, stay in school, and engage in learning when they perceive feeling competent.

Competence and the flex time model: during all interviews with students, teachers, and administrators in Bastoni's (2019) study, it became evident flex time impacted academics in a positive way. One student reported,

> I know some good athletes that don't have the greatest grades but when it comes down to sports and all that stuff they want to play. So, they use the [flex] time to catch up and get their grades up so they can play sports.

Although no students interviewed specifically used the word "competence," students in Bastoni's (2019) study shared that flex time provided time for activities, such as time to work on homework, which resulted in more time to participate in work or recreational activities after school, write college essays, conference with teachers, learn new things through enrichment activities, retake assessments, and participate in Honors classes. In total, students described flex time as time that provided increased opportunities to achieve academic success.

It is important to note SDT does not relate competence to how well a student performs on a specific assignment but instead describes competence as how comfortable an individual feels navigating an environment and moving toward success. For example, one student explained:

> I think [the school created flex time] because some students were complaining . . . falling behind, and they just feel like they have too much work that they can't get done. And so maybe they brought that in to help reduce the workload of students, or to help them, not cope, because cope is too morbid of a word, but help them with managing their workload, whether that be through getting it done in school.

Students also expressed an appreciation of the difference in the structure of flex time compared to the traditional classroom because they could learn in less formal ways, such as working in small groups or getting one-on-one help from a teacher (Bastoni, 2019). As one student said, flex time is helpful because teachers "aren't doing lessons on the board, they're helping you with your work." Another student said:

> If you're behind on a summative, or any test, you can most likely find that class any day of the week and you can sign up for it and you will go in and get help from that teacher. It might not always be one-on-one, but you will get help with *that* teacher.

These quotes depict strong connections between the flex time model and the SDT components of autonomy and competence. Clearly this student appreciated choosing the teacher with whom she would work and felt an increased sense of competence because flex time provided her time to finish her work.

In Bastoni's (2019) study, a few students described how they used this flex time but also articulated positive feelings that stemmed from feelings of competence generated during flex time. As one student shared, "Usually after getting an assignment turned in, after working on it during [flex time]. It's like an accomplishment, so you feel good that you did it."

Through the interview process, teachers' and administrators' responses continuously supported the idea flex time supported the characteristics of SDT (Bastoni, 2019). For example, one teacher said the flex time model had an overall "net positive" impact on the school:

> I think it's great because I teach an AP class. I teach a handful of Honors classes in physics, which are 11th and 12th graders, so I get kids who need time to do reassessment work. I have kids who come in and ask questions. I tell my AP kids that their best thing they can do is sign up every day and just sit and work.

Another teacher illustrated the connections between the flex time model and the SDT:

> I think academic wise having that chance to kind of catch students before they fall through the cracks is good, and then in the more human sense, getting to know our kids on a different level. And I think they trust us a little more because they know that we're giving them opportunities to be successful.

In Bastoni's (2019) study, administrators positively described the connections between the flex time model and the SDT, with one administrator saying,

> I think it's one of those outside the box sort of ideas that has had a pretty decent impact on our learning. Otherwise I don't know when we'd get 670 kids to go to a teacher and get extra help.

According to students, teachers, and administrators, flex time not only increased feelings of competence but also mitigated factors that could otherwise reduce opportunities for students to experience competence, such as a student working after school and participating in sports or other after school activities (Bastoni, 2019). Unique to this high school, the fact that one of the towns in the district does not offer a late bus means students who might want to stay after school cannot access transportation to home.

Questions to ask about competence: competence is one of the key tenets of SDT, and an increase in feelings of competence for students and teachers is one of the major outcomes of the flex time model. Creating time for students to be more successful in school is one of the easiest aspects of the flex time model for most educational stakeholders to understand. However, there may be members of this community who believe students will not use flex time effectively. They might argue students will waste time and goof off. It is therefore important to understand the role competence already plays at your school, what stakeholders' understanding of competence is, and what potential barriers might exist. Spend some time thinking about and taking notes on the following questions:

- How would you describe competence to a parent? A teacher? A school board member? Why do you believe it is important? How would you sell it?
- Does your school value competence for all students? Why or why not?
- What activities/supports do you have in place at your school to increase students' feelings of competence?
- Do teachers feel competent? What support might they need to feel they can help all students learn?
- What would you say to a teacher who thinks students would not do work during flex time?
- What barriers exist in your school that impact students' feeling a sense of competency?
- What stakeholders would work with you to increase feelings of competence for the adults and students at your school?

Relatedness

The last key factor outlined in SDT is relatedness. Relatedness can be understood as valuing and/or developing warmth, understanding, empathy, and trust in the learning environment. To feel secure enough to risk making mistakes and thus engage in real learning, all people need secure and trusting relationships (Deci et al., 2013). To increase students' ability to learn, Cornelius-White (2007) found that teachers must demonstrate they care about each student as a person.

Students who feel respected and welcomed as individuals and cared about by their teachers and peers feel safer, are more likely to engage in learning, and do better academically (Sousa, 2016). After 15 years of analyzing the research on teaching and learning, Hattie (2009) surmised the "optimal classroom climate for learning is one that generates an atmosphere of trust" (p. 29). Hattie (2009) also asserted teacher-student relationships dramatically impact classroom management: "[In] person-centered [classrooms] . . . there is more engagement, more respect of self and others, there are fewer resistant behaviors, there is greater non-directivity [student-initiated and student-regulated activities], and there are higher achievement outcomes" (p. 119).

Research on learning and the brain has reinforced the idea students cannot learn if they do not feel safe. For example, when students feel stress or fear in a learning environment, their brains flood with the chemical cortisol, and they enter "fight or flight" mode. When a student feels threatened or has negative emotions in a classroom, the body activates a rush of adrenaline. Sousa (2016) stated, "This is a reflexive response that shuts down all unnecessary activity and directs the brain's attention to the source of the stimulus" (p. 50).

In both cases, students lose the ability to learn and begin to associate the environment around them with negative feelings. Conversely, when students associate learning environments or teachers with positive feelings, endorphins are released. Endorphins are chemicals that make a student feel good and stimulate learning (Sousa, 2016). From a purely biological perspective, teachers can increase students' ability to focus on learning by ensuring they are teaching in learning environments where students feel safe and by fostering social connections that increase positive feelings of relatedness for all students.

When students learn in environments that do not meet their need for autonomy or relatedness, they often express their feelings through "defiance, power struggles, and disengagement" (Rubin, 2012, pp. 43–44). Students who are disengaged from learning are far more likely to be disruptive (Brophy, 2010; Rubin, 2012). In a report from the UCLA Center for Mental Health in Schools Program and Policy Analysis (2011), researchers found that engagement is associated with positive academic outcomes and is higher when students feel supported by, or can relate to, teachers and peers, while "disengagement from classroom learning is associated with threats to feelings of competence, self-determination, and/or relatedness to valued others" (p. 2).

When schools create learning environments that foster positive peer-to-peer and student-to-teacher relationships, they increase students' ability to feel safe and secure and, in turn, help students develop prosocial values and actions. Conversely, when students do not perceive positive feelings of relatedness at school, they are more likely to be tardy or absent and, ultimately, run an increased risk for dropping out. Sousa (2016) said, "The brain first reacts emotionally to new learning. . . . Thus, any new strategy that generates positive emotions about new learning is a valuable tool to help get and keep students engaged and interested" (p. 135).

Relatedness and the flex time model: every student from Bastoni's (2019) study on the flex time model commented on how flex time played a role in facilitating positive relationships throughout the school. For example, a senior student said:

> [Flex time] helped me a lot because when I was pregnant last year, we had found a lady . . . [that a counselor] brought in . . . me and my boyfriend went together . . . she taught us all about pregnancy and what was happening . . . she gave us good ways to relate to what was going on and helped us learn about it a lot and it helped.

Another senior reflected on a support group in which she participated during flex time as a freshman:

> So, basically, all the girls in my grade would go, for the most part. A lot of us would go. We would talk about either issue we had with each other, with teachers, stuff like that. It really helped our grade . . . all the girls get along, and we don't really get into a lot of drama.

Administrators highlighted the importance of flex time to address the social, emotional, and relational needs of the students as well. One administrator said:

> It feels like in 25 years, kids are just getting more incredibly mentally ill, and we just don't have the supports that we need to provide the services to these families that, on so many levels, have so many needs. . . . When those kids are up here [during flex time] they're in our office getting. . . . I have a basket of granola bars behind you. I have juice in my refrigerator. We've got coffee. Peanut butter crackers. And they just need somebody to just kind of vent out their week and of how they spent it.
>
> But then also, we're developing groups and looking at what services can we provide for those kids. We've connected with two local mental health centers to come in and meet with our kids because they don't have transportation to a mental health center for counseling.

During the interviews for the study, students, teachers, and administrators mentioned flex time also created space for choice over the teacher with whom a student worked, and, through this choice, students and teachers built stronger relationships or learned material in a more comfortable way. For example, a sophomore student said, "Because you're in [flex time] when it's not exactly class time, so you have more time to ask questions and they [the teachers] can see more of who you are."

One teacher reiterated this concept by describing how flex time positively impacted students' ability to choose where they wanted to learn (autonomy) and with whom they wanted to learn (relatedness):

> Maybe one of us has [a specific student] as their grade book teacher, but they get along better with the other [teacher] or they just are able to hear the advice of the other [teacher] a little bit better, [flex time] helps them get the help they need. Or even like sometimes kids just don't want to go to the person who grades them to get feedback before they turn something in.

Another teacher explained the benefits of flex time for relationship building this way:

> Everybody raises their hand at once in class. I'm like a pinball machine, whereas with [flex time is] more one-on-one time with kids. Not only am I helping them academically, we're also building relationships with them, also, getting to know them because they might not talk in front of a full class of kids, but they'll talk to me [during flex time].

During the interviews, students and teachers also mentioned relationships were built during flex time, in part because they could do things together that were not graded (Bastoni, 2019). In one classroom, a teacher described how she formed an unexpected positive relationship with some students in her advisory, and the students ended up choosing to be in her room for most of flex time. Over time, this teacher said she grew to "love" these students, even though they were difficult. She felt she became a mentor to them and provided them with nonacademic items they needed. She shared:

> There's no grade associated [with flex time]. . . . So, I could have these conversations . . . I was able to have some great discussions with them about what it means to, like, mature. About why what they just said was inappropriate. And, I'll be honest, there was one kid in there who—he's a senior—and I still worry if he's going to graduate or drop out, or whatever. But, I could discretely feed him every day [during flex time].

By providing snacks, this teacher built relationships with students outside of the academic setting. In Bastoni's (2019) study, students reported flex time facilitated relationship building because it allowed them to see their friends. Students particularly appreciated this when they did not share class with a particular friend. For example, a sophomore student said, "This morning, cursive was fun 'cause I was with all my friends. Some teachers do games, so we sign up for those." Or, as her friend said,

> Sometimes, if I don't have any other homework, I play games with my friends, like card games . . . I can sign up for my Spanish teacher and me and a group of my friends, we all get together to play . . . that's my favorite part.

Another sophomore student explained how flex time allows for relationship building:

> If you don't have that teacher as one of your teachers and you wanted to get to know them or you knew them a few years ago or something like that you can sign up for them . . . I also like how you're mixed with pretty much any grade level so you obviously get to meet new people that way.

Teachers and students also commented on how flex time allowed students to feel more comfortable asking questions (Bastoni, 2019). Both students and teachers described students feeling more secure asking questions during flex time because the setting was smaller and less intimidating. This outcome can be understood as a connection to relatedness and competence, because it not only allows additional time for students to get answers to questions but also positively increases students' feelings of being understood and valued.

Teachers also felt flex time provided a space where they could demonstrate care for a student by making the learning environment less stressful for them. "I would just feel nervous to raise their hand in class because they don't want a student to see their weakness. And [flex time] is a great opportunity for the student to get help one-on-one," explained a teacher as flex time was taking place.

As a teacher across the hall said, "Kids, they just felt stupid in front of the class. But at least when it was in here [during flex time] they knew they could ask me, and their peers weren't leering at them." Many students shared this same feeling. Another student shared, "It's easier because when you ask a teacher questions in [flex time] they can answer it but sometimes they can't in class because there's other kids in there."

Although students' experiences of relatedness varied—as some used the time to connect with peers, some used the time to connect to teachers, and some gathered social or emotional supports—it is clear one of the positive outcomes of flex time overall was an increase in feelings of relatedness.

Questions to ask about relatedness: relatedness is one of the key tenets of SDT, and an increase in feelings of relatedness for students and teachers is one of the major outcomes of the flex time model. It is important to understand the role relatedness already plays at your school, what the perceptions of relatedness are, and what potential barriers might exist. Spend some time thinking about and taking notes on the following questions:

- How would you describe the importance of relatedness to a parent? A teacher? A school board member? Why do you believe it is important? How would you sell it?
- Does your school value relationships/relatedness for all students? Why or why not?
- What activities/supports do you have at your school to increase students' feelings of relatedness?
- Do teachers feel positive feelings of relatedness? What supports might they need?
- What stakeholders would work with you to increase feelings of relatedness for the adults and students at your school?

JESSICA'S STORY

My name is Jessica, and I started high school in Fall 2014. Coming to high school was a rough but meaningful transition. It is very difficult to switch school systems as an upperclassman, but it was even more difficult to change geographic locations. I was born and raised in Cape Cod, MA. After living in two foster homes, I moved from Cape Cod, MA, to Greenfield, NH, where I would start and finish my last 2 years of high school. According to my social worker at the time, the idea behind moving all that distance was to ensure I was living in a placement suitable for my many needs.

Teenage years are never easy, and being in a placement exacerbated normal teenage barriers. When I found out I had to move and change schools, I felt very frustrated and hurt. Because of this, I did not have the highest expectations. Truth be told, I did not want to be there. I did not want to move. I did not want any part of these substantial changes taking place in my life without my permission.

I have spastic quadriplegic cerebral palsy, so not only was I set up to be "the new girl" in a new town, a new state, and a new living environment, I was also "the new girl with a disability" who stuck out like a sore thumb. However, I did not want to become more of an outcast by isolating myself, so I put myself out there with the intention to be known as more than just the disabled new girl. Joining extracurricular activities, such as the school yearbook and newspaper, gave me a sense of confidence and allowed me to feel I was not confined to society's labels.

Yes, I was the new girl. Yes, I had a disability. But, I was also the social media editor of the yearbook and a writer for the school newspaper. Both clubs met during flex time, which was perfect for me because I had to take a special bus home to my placement site and would not have been able to participate if the meetings had not occurred during the school day.

A few months later, my newly found sense of confidence seemed to deteriorate rapidly, as one thing after another reared its ugly head in my life. There was no specific event but rather a layering of events, a snowball effect that caused me to develop suicidal ideations. At first, I was very embarrassed to learn the school had been contacted and knew how I was feeling. For me, I believed my own personal issues should stay personal and not be brought into the school environment. I thought getting the school involved was one of the worst plans of action to take, but, in reality, it ended up being one of the best.

The school psychologist recommended I attend Zen Den, a meditation group, which met during flex time, to enhance the social and emotional well-being of students through mindfulness. The instructor of the group, one of the two student assistance counselors, would sometimes perform Reiki on us. When I was growing up, my mother used to pay out of pocket for me to receive Reiki treatments, and, here I was at school, experiencing the benefits of Reiki free of charge.

After being suicidal my junior year, I really wanted to take time in my senior year to establish what I had learned about myself mentally and emotionally and use it to inspire others. The director of school counseling offered me a life-changing opportunity to speak at a community panel on teenage depression. It was the first time I had spoken openly in front of a group of people about something so deep and personal to me.

I believe that was the first step to having many more open discussions I would grow to love and enjoy. It drove a lasting desire in me to want to advocate for mental health issues and ensure those who are struggling get the treatment they need. I did not just want to stop there and felt there was more I could do, especially being a high school student who experienced the effects of mental illness firsthand.

In an attempt to find other healthy ways to deliver my message, I met with the student assistance counselor. I shared the same testimony with her I had given at the community panel, and she encouraged me to think about becoming a peer educator in the school's Signs of Suicide program. To do this, I accompanied two student assistant counselors as they led a discussion during flex time that educated freshman students on warning signs and misconceptions about suicide. From there, I shared my story with students and provided them with onsite resources they might use if they, a classmate, or a friend needed help.

Students took depression/anxiety screenings that day, and it is my hope this program helped students who needed support. I know it would have made a huge difference for me during my battle with depression to have a safe space in school to initiate this dialogue, and I am very blessed I potentially could be that person for somebody else in need.

Another opportunity in which I chose to engage more deeply was the student leadership team, or Student Organization United in Leadership (SOUL), which again met during flex time. It was through SOUL that other members and I organized a Spirit of Kindness week to shed light on the many different struggles students in today's society face. With a fellow student and friend, we gave an "FTM talk" about our experiences with depression.

The FTM talks are similar to TED talks, and anybody—students and staff alike—could schedule themselves to hear these presentations from local professionals. At the end, we passed out sticky notes to members of the audience so they could ask questions or give feedback. I still have some of the sticky notes we received from audience members with encouraging messages of love and support. They are displayed on my mirror, and, when I am having a tough day, I can look at them and remember what a large impact something small can have on yourself and others. Other speakers for Spirit of Kindness came from all over the region and all different walks of life, including the guest speaker who advocated for substance abuse recovery and another guest speaker who addressed his journey defeating body image issues and how turning to mindfulness helped him cope with difficult challenges.

The substance abuse speaker's message was particularly meaningful to me, as the same year I heard his presentation, I lost my sister to substance abuse. She had endocarditis, an infection in the heart valves caused by the injection of drugs with contaminated needles. She was hospitalized in a coma and deemed incapacitated, meaning she was too sick to effectively make her own decisions about health and treatment.

Due to this, I used flex time as a time to receive emotional support from school counselors and occasionally speak with medical professionals by phone about my sister's case. During this difficult time, school leaders supported me in arranging transportation to Massachusetts to visit my sister by advocating for me and speaking on my behalf with the appropriate channels at Crotched Mountain.

In the last couple months of my sister's life, the hospital requested somebody step in as a court-appointed guardian. I really wanted to do this for my sister, as I felt I did not have much control over what was happening, but I could take on the role of guardian to put some control back into her life and be a voice for her when she was unable to speak for herself. Thanks to flex time, I was able to attend a court hearing by phone and was granted joint guardianship of my sister with a court-appointed lawyer.

Through flex time, I could take care of personal issues without them interfering too heavily with schoolwork and my education. By the time my sister passed away, I was definitely a well-versed user of flex time. To me, flex time is all about offering a space to create balance in your life.

Most often, I decided how I spent my time during flex time, depending on the circumstances, even if it meant using it to lie down and take a nap. If I only slept 2 hours the previous night, my class performance would be affected if I did not take time to rest. Independently managing my flex time was a great way to prepare me for college and adulthood. It taught me to use my time wisely and sufficiently but also take responsibility for my actions and how they impact my future. It enabled me to succeed in more ways than one and allotted me the time to explore different academic, social, and health-related activities.

While I used the flex time for extracurricular activities like SOUL, I could also use the time to work on school assignments. My placement was a medical group home facility, which was not always an ideal environment to complete homework assignments, as they served individuals with a wide range of disabilities, including behavioral disabilities. This could be distracting at times, and flex time helped me stay on top of my schoolwork and gave me time to meet with various school-based health professionals to receive disability services. I received physical, occupational, and vision therapy during flex time, which eliminated being pulled out of class and missing important lectures or material.

For as long as I can remember, I struggled in math, and, in 2014, I was diagnosed with a math-related learning disability called nonverbal learning disorder. My school counselor helped to coordinate my meeting with a tutor on a weekly basis during flex time to help ensure I could pass the Accuplacer for college. With the help and support of my tutor and math teacher, I passed the Accuplacer successfully and was accepted into Eastern Nazarene College.

I would not have been able to attend Eastern Nazarene College if not for Dollars for Scholars, a community-based scholarship of which I was blessed to be a recipient. When I graduated in 2016, it was easily one of the most exciting and rewarding days of my life. I also credit flex time for helping me prepare for graduation by giving me time to practice walking in the walker with my physical therapists.

Many factors have contributed to the success I have experienced but none more so than flex time. It does not matter what area of your life needs enrichment—if you use the time wisely, it will help you. I know I am not the only student who has a heavy load of things to handle beyond the hours of a typical school day, and I cannot stress enough how the 40 minutes of flex time allowed me to handle what I may have not been able to otherwise.

Jessica's statement is strong and is one example of how flex time can contribute to a positive school culture. Other students also used flex time to personalize their educational experience by building on their strengths and getting the additional support in areas that may be a weakness. This all culminated together to improve overall school culture.

Jessica's story gives us unique insight into students' learning experiences in the flex time model. Jessica's story demonstrates how flex time provided one student with feelings of autonomy, relatedness, and competence. Spend some time thinking about and taking notes on the following questions:

- How do you think the flex time model improved Jessica's experience in high school?
- What parts of Jessica's story relate to your school?
- Where in Jessica's story do you see her experiencing competence, relatedness, or autonomy?
- How could Jessica's story inform the decisions you make at your school?

BILL LEAHY'S PERSPECTIVE

School culture monitor, Bill Leahy, had the following to say about flex time:

During my time as an educator, I worked in two high schools that used the flex time model. At one of these high schools, I worked as a career and technical education (CTE) paraprofessional, and I was a culture monitor at the other. Both of these jobs allowed me great amounts of freedom—perhaps more freedom than any other staff member. Through these positions, I had the flexibility to establish relationships with students, find out what they needed for support, and help them be successful.

Most importantly, flex time gave me the opportunity to make connections, give encouragement, and serve as a role model and mentor. I really enjoyed these aspects of my positions—for me, it was payback. When I was a senior in high school, I lacked direction and was confused. After a night of partying, I was in my advanced math class with my head on the desk falling asleep. Mr. G, my math teacher, tapped me on the arm, and when I looked up bleary eyed and in a fog, he just said, "If you need someone to talk to, I'm available." I never took him up on it, but I knew he cared. To this day, I remember it as a very important instance of encouragement in my life.

Many of the students with whom I worked at both schools were at high risk for failure. As a culture monitor, we identified students at risk through a data system that tracked behavior referrals. The top 5% of students accounted for over 50% of discipline issues. Counselors, social workers, admin, and support staff met weekly to develop plans to support these students socially, emotionally, and academically. The flex time allowed flexibility as we developed creative ways to help these students.

I would do "check ins" with a number of students and meet with students in my office, the library, or at whatever class they had selected for their flex time. One important benefit of the flex time model is I did not have to interrupt a regular class to meet with students.

The flex time was also a great help in mentoring students through a program out of the University of New Hampshire that was student centered and involved goal setting, identifying resources, and having students choose the people who could help support them in achieving their goals. Two students I mentored through to graduation really stuck out to me: Robbie and Merrick. I helped both students using flex time. Together we did goal setting, researched resources, and set up meetings in and out of school with those whom they identified as supportive people in their lives.

In Robbie's case, he struggled to achieve his goals, but I could see how much the relationship and support meant to him. He matured, grew in responsibility, and developed closer relationships with those whom he had identified as supports. Merrick was more successful in achieving his goals and went on to postsecondary education and training. Although the outcomes were different for Robbie and Merrick, the flex time helped both students mature, develop a sense of belonging, and realize they could find their own autonomy.

While at one high school, I also used flex time as a means to connect and support members of the alpine ski team I coached. I supported them when academic eligibility or behavioral issues came up and once again to establish connections and supportive relationships. They were not students with a high risk for failure, and yet they benefited from the attention I gave during flex time.

I also helped with hallway supervision during times I was not meeting with students. To be honest, it was the least enjoyable aspect of my job, yet I could see how keeping disruption to a minimum greatly benefitted the students who were engaged during the flex time. Many students said the flex time model was a great help academically and was so important for dealing with their busy schedules. The benefits of this time for a large majority of students far outweighed organizing and managing sometimes reluctant students.

While working as a CTE paraprofessional, I had the same goals of relationship building and connecting with students. This worked out in different ways because they were different schools, and I had a different position at each. Through flex

Step 1: Make a Philosophical Shift—Implementation

time at this high school, I developed these relationships because I could interact more frequently with students and help with academics more because I was in an assist role in their classes. Because I co-led an advisory group with Jenny, an administrative assistant, we had daily contact with the same students and built relationships more quickly with a diverse group of students.

One of the goals of the advisory group was to support, encourage, and mentor nontraditional students in the CTE program. We were specifically interested in developing support for English language learners in these programs by providing social, emotional, and academic support. Relationship building included everything from discussing the latest NBA scores and games to selecting prom dresses. Support varied from vocabulary development to the technical components of CTE courses such as automotive, electricity, robotics, and other courses in the program. The connections and relationships we established were pivotal to getting these students to take risks and build confidence.

Because I worked as a CTE paraprofessional in a number of classrooms, I was able to better support students with their projects and assignments. Whether it be a graphic design or intro to marketing course, for example, I could coordinate with the students' teachers, and we could assist the students who needed support in a more focused and effective manner.

Flex time is very beneficial for academic learning and achievement. It helps students to learn for a variety of reasons. Of greater benefit is the development of relationships and connections. When I look back at the many students I got to know and help, I hope at least a few felt I was one of the people who "tapped them on the arm" and encouraged them to succeed.

SCHOOL CULTURE: THE KEY TO SUCCESS AND HOW FLEX TIME HELPS IT IMPROVE!

A culture is not a piece of a school's success, but it is the foundation of its success. In fall of 2016, a flex time model school had the privilege of having Australian exchange students and staff visit the school for a few days and experience the U.S. education system. One of the Australian teachers had the following to say in his daily blog about the school's culture:

> When you walk the hallways of this high school, exchange teachers from Austria quickly develop a sense of envy because the school's atmosphere is so

very friendly, but above all respectful and inclusive. Compared to high schools in Austria, this FTM school is very well equipped for instruction in all subject areas. It is possible, and indeed customary, to engage students in practical applications of their learning.

By looking at figure 1.1, one can see student discipline data from one flex time model school decreased significantly. This student discipline data directly connect to this school's positive increase in school culture, which creates a school where students want to be. This is exciting for all school stakeholders.

Most individuals have grown up in brick-and-mortar schools with traditional scheduling models that group students into categories based on seat time credits with a prescribed curriculum that does not account for individual needs and strengths. While this works for some students, it does not allow for personalized learning, which provides students what they need in a timely manner and the opportunity to be exactly who they are. Traditional school systems had their purpose, but traditional schools are not meeting many students' needs today.

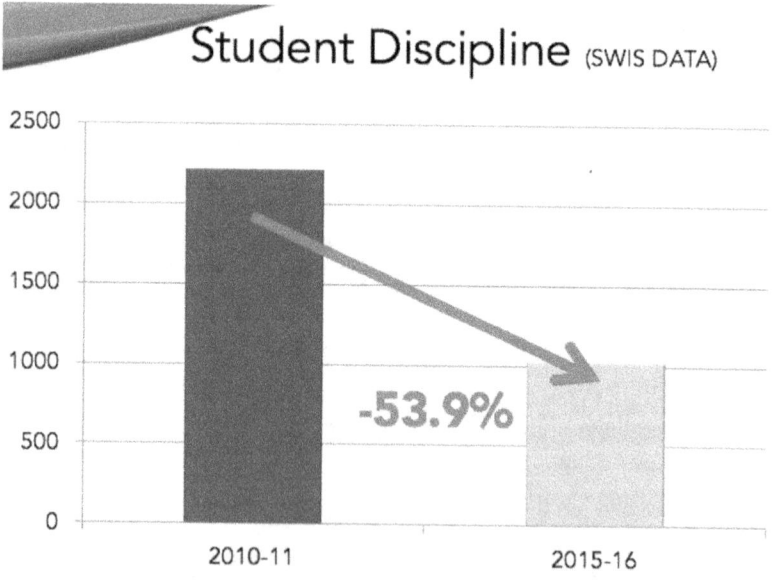

Figure 1.1 **Student discipline data.** *Source*: Author image.

Empowering and engaging our students by supporting academic success, allowing them time to tap into their passions, supporting their social and emotional needs during times of struggle, and modeling kindness gives students their best chance for a positive culture for learning. Flex time allows much of that to happen, and modeling positive behavior is a constant practice that becomes a habit for the entire school community.

Flexible scheduling and school culture work hand in hand. Schools with flex time offer students the opportunity to engage in learning activities they could never access in a traditional schedule. Flex time also allows students a chance to breathe and balance their day to complete some homework in school and not in the evening at home where the environments are not necessarily conducive to learning. Instead of sitting in course after course with work piling up that needs to be completed at home, students now can spend that time working on the material that needs to be completed and do so with a teacher who can best support them.

Students can also use their time to work on their passions by either extending their learning in courses they love or creating new enrichment activities in partnership with their teachers. Students and teachers can engage in their passions, and students can get creative without any administrative directives. For example, some enrichment activities might include the German teacher and a math teacher partnering for German math games, the chemistry and art teachers partnering for projects stimulated by a guest speaker, and students meeting with a local construction manager. In the past, principals have had to say "no" to requests for guest speakers or activities that pulled students out of their classes, but, with flex time, that does not happen.

Students become passionate about their flex time and find a sense of balance between instructional time and individually constructed time. Every student begins to find their own balance between enrichment time and extra help that fits their needs in a given week. The teachers help with these decisions when students need a boost! This personalized culture supports the self-advocating skill and independence that students need in postsecondary education or careers but with careful monitoring and direction. We are giving up some control and supporting independence but also recognize we are guiding teenage learners, and the system and technology to manage it allows teachers to be directive when needed, knowing the mission for most schools is learning for all.

Teachers have the opportunity to leap into their passions during flex time like never before. They can offer extended learning opportunities (ELOs) that connect to their personal passions and be creative while doing this. They can help students one on one and spend time in professional learning communities during the school day. Teachers can provide further opportunities that would never have been possible in the traditional system. When our teachers are creative and spread their wings, students experience their energy and begin to fly as well.

A culture that supports success is flexible, inviting, and ready to stimulate creative minds for both students and teachers. If you can create a school where students want to be, you can create a school for students that is fun, stimulating, and successful.

Chapter 2

Step 2: Understand the Structure—Implementation

Create Space, Not Limitations

While there are many iterations of the flex time model, the origins of the model began with Brian Pickering, former principal of a high school in Peterborough, NH, and the 2016 New Hampshire Association of Secondary Schools Principal of the Year. The idea for the model began in 2010 when Pickering felt he was unable to provide additional academic help for a student who was involved in numerous after-school activities. The student was at a loss for how to get the help she needed because her teacher could not come before school, the student could not meet after school, and they did not have a shared lunch. Pickering found it difficult to carve out time for supports and enrichment activities and engaged a team of teachers, staff, and students to brainstorm solutions. They eventually created the flex time model.

The flex time model is a school structure that provides a set amount of time each school day during which students have control over where they go and what they do. This amount of time can vary and typically ranges from 30 to 60 minutes. During flex time, attendance is taken, and students are required to be actively working; however, they have choices over what they work on and where they work. This autonomy gives students control and choice.

For example, students who are doing well in school can choose to participate in enrichment activities, students who are struggling can choose to get extra help, and students who need social or emotional assistance can choose to participate in counseling sessions. A chemistry teacher at a high school in New Hampshire, Moria Milne, said freedom of choice "allowed these curious students to plan, setup, and conduct experiments of their own choosing." She continued, "Often, other [flex time] students become drawn into activities happening at the lab bench, and before we know it, we've all learned something new and memorable."

At this high school, students who are struggling in class can be prescheduled by a teacher, but they can only be prescheduled for two flex time blocks per week; thus, they retain some control over how they spend their time. Additionally, students regain control over their schedule once they are doing better in the class. According to Pickering, the flex time model has some things in common with study halls, advisories, extra classes, and after-school help sessions but offers more than any of those single interventions.

Students can use the time to read, work on homework, study, work out, or work in the art room. Students can select where they want to work, what they want to work on, and, by doing so, improve academic and personal goals. One administrator at a school using the flex time model described the block this way:

> It's a time for students to do enrichment, intervention, Honors work. There's no public transportation. So, we were finding kids couldn't stay after school for extra help. So, embedding it during the day allows equal access for everybody to the teachers and for that intervention time as well as for kids who want to take a lesson to a different level.

At Pickering's high school in New Hampshire, a school that uses the flex time model, 43 minutes are set aside for flex time. Each Monday, a homeroom mentor works with a set cohort of students to schedule where they would like to work for the upcoming week. This mentor works with these students for 4 years. Students can also adjust their schedules as needed during the week, but having a weekly meeting allows the teacher to monitor grades and advise students.

Teachers still have a scheduled prep time, and they are not expected to create lesson plans for flex time. According to Pickering, the goal of flex time is to give students control of how they spend their time during the regular school day. The flex time model supports student autonomy because students can choose how to use the time they are given, as noted by the high school's band director. He described how he sees student autonomy play out in his classroom:

> It is a good feeling for me when, during [flex time], unprompted by my direction, I hear trumpets practicing the music I gave them in second block, a tenor

sax practicing a jazz band solo, a drummer learning piano, and a History of Rock [course] student making up a quiz for a higher grade. [This time] is an organized smorgasbord of high levels of learning.

Pickering reported that, after implementing the flex time model, his high school saw a 53% drop in behavioral referrals. This may be related to the increase in autonomy the flex time model provides, since, when students feel they have more autonomy, they are less likely to participate in combative behaviors, more likely to engage in learning, and feel better about themselves overall (Rubin, 2012). Increases in autonomy are not only associated with increases in learning but also positively impact well-being (Deci et al., 1996; Grolnick & Ryan, 1987).

Before implementing the flex time model, Guy Donnelly, a high school principal, reported that attendance rates were below 89%; now they are at 93%, which is above the state average (Pickering & Bastoni, 2016). This result may be due to the relationship between SDT and the flex time model, since research has demonstrated a strong link between increases in SDT-supportive environments, student enjoyment of learning, and intrinsic motivation, and a decrease in students' likelihood of dropping out of school (Akram et al., 2014; Deci et al., 1996). A research team found "any input that is experienced as support for autonomy enhances intrinsic motivation, whereas any that is experienced as a controller of behavior thwarts satisfaction of the need for autonomy and decreases intrinsic motivation" (Deci et al., 1996, p. 174).

THE FLEX TIME MODEL IN PRACTICE

Figure 2.1 is a detailed description of what happens in one of the flex time rooms. Here is what the flex time model might look like in practice.

At the beginning of flex time, after taking attendance and greeting students in a friendly, inviting manner, a teacher asks a specific student to come up to her desk. The teacher shows the student his grade in another class and asks if he has spoken with the teacher about the grade. The student says he has not. The teacher then lists potential ways the student could improve his grade and even issues the student a pass to see the teacher in another flex time classroom to discuss, in person, ways he could improve his grade. Although the student is initially resistant, the teacher kindly but directly pushes the student to

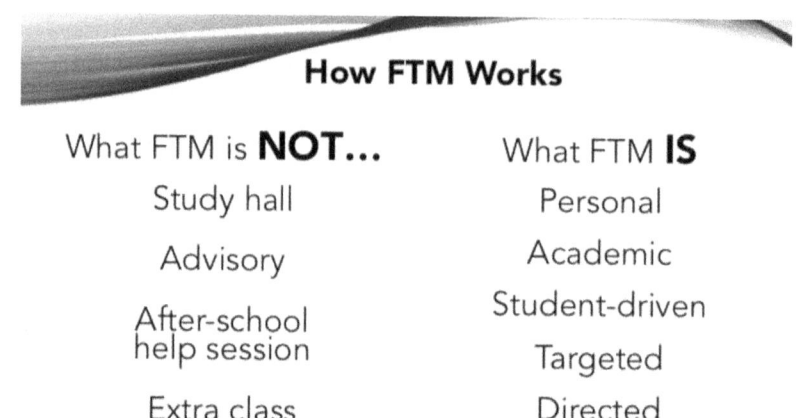

Figure 2.1 **How the flex time model works.** *Source*: Author image.

inquire what could be done to improve the grade. Finally, the student agrees that talking with the other teacher makes sense, accepts the pass his flex time teacher provides him, and speaks with the other teacher.

The student leaves and returns very quickly, reporting the teacher with whom they needed to meet was absent. The flex time teacher then asks the student if he would like her to discuss his grade and potential options for improving it with the other teacher to learn what the student could do. The student says "yes" and thanks the teacher. He then sits down, reporting to his flex time teacher he needs to finish some work for another class.

For the rest of flex time, the teacher moves between two groups of students. Two female students sit at one table quietly working. One of the young women asks the teacher to look at an assignment she submitted for the teacher's class but on which she did not receive a good grade. The teacher moves toward the student to answer her questions but first redirects a group of young men who are not engaged in any observable academic work. The teacher then provides very specific one-on-one help to the young woman who wants to improve her grade. After reexplaining a concept related to the student's specific question, the teacher kneels beside the student's desk and asks her if she understands the rest of the homework.

Periodically, while working with this student, the teacher looks up and calmly asks the group of young men what they were working on. After a few minutes, the young men pull out Chromebooks and can be heard asking each other questions about a shared homework assignment. For the rest of flex time, the teacher moves between these two groups, completely absorbed in answering questions and keeping students on task. After the initial movement of students coming into the room or leaving to go to preassigned activities in other locations, the room is quiet and there is a general air of work being done. Students do not line up at the door and do not stop working until the block is over.

After analyzing how time is spent by both teachers and students during flex time, in this room, in the hallways, and in other rooms, it is evident the majority of students were engaged in activities related to academics (competency-based activities) or fun activities (some of which were relational). Out of the observed flex time blocks in Bastoni's (2019) study, 30% of students were seen engaged in academic pursuits, such as doing homework, redoing assessments, and completing missing work. Forty-four percent of the students were seen engaged in activities categorized as fun or relational, which included playing cards, participating in enrichment activities, such as practicing cursive writing on a large blackboard, or engaging with their peers in work for specific student-oriented clubs. The remaining students, approximately 25%, were seen taking breaks, which included talking with friends with no observable academic purpose, waiting in line at the coffee shop, or using their phones. Again, none of the students were disruptive, and no disciplinary activity was seen.

The findings from these observations demonstrated direct connections between the SDT characteristics of competence and relatedness, since students were seen involved in activities that served as bonding time with peers and teachers, or they were seen participating in activities that could increase their feelings of competency through increased academic understanding or better grades on homework or assessments in general (Bastoni, 2019). In addition, by spending one-on-one time answering questions, and by conferencing with students to help them find ways to increase their grades (as described in the detailed observation), teachers were clearly creating environments where trust and relatedness were built and competence was developed.

FLEX TIME SCHEDULING THAT FITS

Hundreds of schools across the country have implemented a version of the flex time model. There are no two schools that are exactly the same in how they use this model, but there are several fundamental pieces that are consistent for the success of a school's flex time model. Two of these fundamental elements include the amount of time set aside for flex time and the adult-to-student relationships created with an effective mentor program.

Timing and Mentor Groups

Flex time can occur during the regular school day and can be anywhere from 30 to 43 minutes long. There are some examples of shorter or longer flex times based on the needs of each individual school. Flex time often involves a homeroom mentor and a stable cohort of students for the duration of 4 years. This creates a safe place for students to come together on Mondays to schedule their flex time for the week and connect with students in all grade levels.

Some schools use a different day to meet with their mentors to schedule flex time. These students can be systematically put into their mentor groups through a questionnaire at the end of their eighth-grade school year. Flex time draws on all teachers, paraprofessionals, specialists, school counselors, and administrators to participate in supporting student success. All teachers still have their scheduled prep time, but no staff has this flex time off. During this time, they are actively supporting students in a more open and free-flowing manner.

Types of Flex Time Learning Opportunities

Flex time is for all students and was designed for the entire student body to participate in. Each week, all students can schedule their weekly enrichment activities, extra help, interventions, or supports in partnership with their homeroom teacher and course teachers. If students are struggling in courses, their teachers and/or mentors can preschedule them in those specific classes during the school week. Teacher prescheduling for additional support creates an incentive for students to work hard in their classes so they can use their flex time as needed during a given day or week.

The flex time model empowers students to be in charge of their own learning. Their scheduling is on demand, as they can schedule their flex time on Mondays for the week ahead. Students no longer need to wait for days and often weeks to find an available time to meet with their teachers before school, at lunch, or after school. Flex time allows students to get the help they need when they need it and stay on target in classes. Students are learning to advocate for their success in school, and they have the safety net of their mentors if they do not know how they should be spending their flex time. An additional benefit of flex time is students independently taking ownership of their education. They are gaining and building student autonomy throughout this experience.

What Is and What Is Not Flex Time?

Over the past several years, schools have taken steps to clarify their progressive educational practices with clear views on what flex time is and what it is not. Flex time is not a study hall, advisory, after-school help session, or extra class. These terms are far too generic and misrepresent the flex time model goals. The model is truly a flexible period of time that is personal, academic, student driven, targeted, and directed, as needed.

Each school staff member creates their own use of this time in communication with their students to meet their classroom goals and the overall goals of the school. Staff members make use of their flex time in a manner that supports the well-being and holistic success of all students. Flex time can be represented in many ways throughout the school as seen in figure 2.2. While taking a walk through a flex time school's hallways, it is easy to be amazed

MONDAY	TUESDAY	WEDNESDAY	THURSDAY	FRIDAY
Mentor Mondays	Interventions	Interventions	Interventions	Interventions
	Enrichments	Enrichments	Enrichments	Enrichments
	Extensions	Extensions	Extensions	Extensions
	Supports	Supports	Supports	Supports

Figure 2.2 **Potential structure of an average week.** *Source*: Author image.

by all the focused, innovative, and resilient students and teachers working on their passions and striving for success.

After a few years of flex time in a school, all the expanded opportunities naturally begin to take place. The number of ELOs taking place in many schools brings out burning passions among students. It is not uncommon to see students working after school, not because they have to, but because they want to. They often are not in school working because they have an assignment due the next day but because their passion for the subject is burning so fierce that they cannot get enough of their projects.

ELOs give students the ability to create their own course of study for credit surrounded by real subject matter in a self-focused manner. In the traditional educational model, this would not have been possible in such large numbers. Teachers are grateful and excited to see students loving school and pursuing their interests so intensively (figure 2.3).

Despite what activities are permitted or not, scheduling is the most complicated issue in flex time implementation. Many schools started using Google

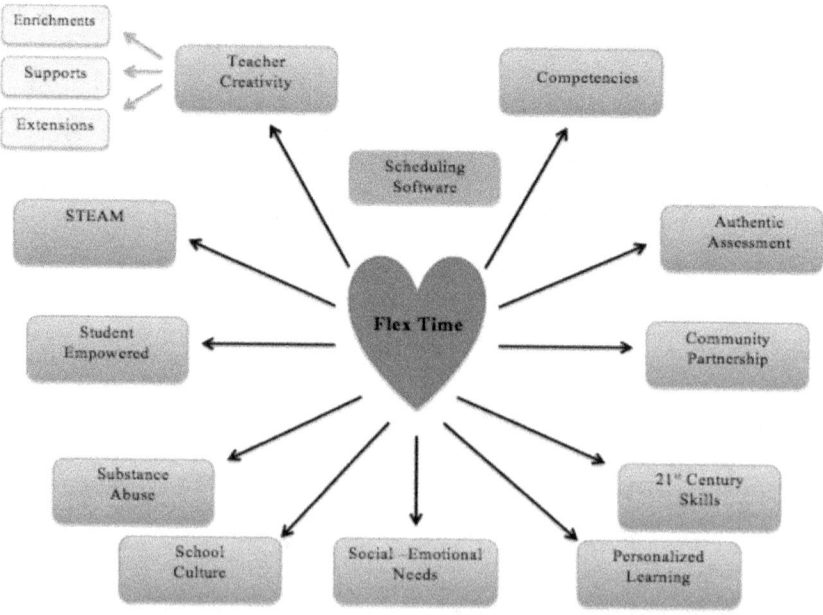

Figure 2.3 **Flex time scheduling.** *Source*: Author image.

Docs for scheduling and reported back quickly that it did not work. Since scheduling is so critical to the effective deployment of the flex time model, schools are encouraged to use scheduling software to ensure scheduling is less cumbersome. The software a school chooses should have a system to record and store data on where and how students are using their flex time, how often, and what they are doing when they arrive. However, whatever scheduling software or practices a school uses, the results of this study emphasize the need for students to have some choice in and ownership of how to use their time.

At some schools with the flex time model, teachers work directly with students on scheduling. At other schools, students directly schedule themselves from an app on their phone or computer. Schools using the flex time model, but giving no scheduling control to students at all, have reported major problems of using the model. When teachers are the only individuals scheduling, the SDT characteristics of relatedness and autonomy are lost. At schools that use flex time in this way, there are very few creative offerings for students during flex time; thus, the positive outcomes associated with fun are also nonexistent.

Over the past 5 years, students, families, and the community have become connected to, and appreciative of, this innovative model in educational practice, and they are thankful to work in partnership with these school stakeholders to support greater levels of success for all children. This journey is much bigger than one high school. It is about creating a model that works for all students. Every flex time model can be different, and that is what is so exciting and special about flex time. Schools have to continue to do what works for their school communities.

At one New Hampshire high school, flex time runs for 40 minutes each day on a 6-day schedule. Flex time takes place after the first block of the day, which lasts for 80 minutes. After the first 80-minute and 40-minute flex time blocks, there are four more 60-minute blocks of class time and one 26-minute block for lunch. The school day starts at 7:20 a.m. and ends at 2:10 p.m.

Flex time is broken into two parts at this school: advisory and flex time. Advisory is when students plan their schedule and meet with a specific teacher in a specific room for the entire year. During advisory, students receive support, and they focus on academic skill building. During advisory, freshman and sophomores participate in activities designed to help with the transition to high school, while juniors and seniors focus on college and career preparedness. Students receive academic credit and a grade for participation in advisory but do not receive a grade or credit for flex time. Freshman and sophomore Honors classes take place during flex time, which runs once during the 6-day schedule.

At the beginning of each scheduling cycle, students are given a calendar of offerings. Using this calendar, students can schedule themselves to specific rooms throughout the school, where they participate in the activities listed. In addition to Honors for freshmen and sophomores, activities include things like cribbage, making dream catchers, open gym, support groups, extra time to work on assignments, clubs, extra help or reteaching, music practice, and drawing. If a student is not doing well in class, needs to retake a summative assessment, or has missed class, teachers can schedule that student to their room.

If a teacher schedules a student, the student cannot override the reschedule, and they are considered booked for that day. During this flex time, students are not required to book their math teacher to get math help. Instead, they can book to any room they feel comfortable in and do their work there. In other words, students can decide whom they want to go to for help but with assistance from the teachers who are working with them on a daily basis.

As a school, discussing goals and priorities for the flex time model is an important part of preparing to get started. Many schools use a one flex block/period in the middle of the day, others prefer one at the beginning or end of the day, some have rotating schedules to match their rotating days, and others have multiple flex blocks/periods or even whole-day flex times. Figure 2.4

Sample School 1	Sample School 2
Block 1	Block 1
FTM (41 minutes)	Block 2
Block 2	FTM (45 minutes)
Block 3	Block 3
Block 4	Block 4

Figure 2.4 Common flex time schedules at sample high schools. *Source*: Enriching Students—model example.

includes models from real schools across the country that use a format that fits their community best.

As you can see in figure 2.4, Sample High School 1 uses the same flex time model as Sample High School 2, but their timings differ, as one schedules their flex time before Block 2 and one school schedules their flex time before Block 3. Other schools run their flex time before Block 1 or after Block 4. There is no one answer to where flex time should be scheduled in your school day.

Some staff may run a teacher and/or student survey to see what their community would prefer, while other teams may choose what would make the most sense based on other school variables. As long as this decision is made by a team, it will work out. Everything can be adjusted as needed. Reflection is important for both the students and staff when making any adjustments.

If we take a look at the flex time schedule in figure 2.5, this high school has two different day schedules that are a regular part of their routine. They run a 45-minute and a 60-minute flex time on differing scheduled days. By looking at the classes and times, one can see a few minutes were shaved from each block, based on the school's original model, to fit their school and community. This is unique to their classes and programs and allows their students to all take advantage of flex time.

One high school in New Hampshire created their model with a focus on three components of their school's overall flex time vision: community, mentoring, and academics. The Sample School 3 started Year 1 with a primary focus on academics to allow students to have time to complete coursework in the school day. They kept their students-per-staff ratio as small as possible.

Sample School 3

45 Minutes FTM

Block 1	(75 minutes)
Block 2: FTM	(45 minutes)
Block 3	(75 minutes)
Block 4	(109 minutes)
Block 5	(75 minutes)

60 Minutes FTM

Block 1	(73 minutes)
Block 2: FTM	(60 minutes)
Block 3	(73 minutes)
Block 4	(100 minutes)
Block 5	(73 minutes)

Figure 2.5 **Example flex time schedule.** *Source*: Enriching Students—model example.

This was in the range of twelve to fifteen students per teacher. They offered some test prep opportunities and science lab opportunities as original extensions (Brown & Hall, 2016).

The Sample School 3 assistant principal, Justin Brown, discussed their school's expansion and growth of the flex time model in their second year. This high school was prescheduling students to get CPR training! It did not stop there, as opportunities established with community partners became available during flex time as well. The school partnered with the University of Vermont staff and students and had guest lecturers speak during flex time about subjects like neuroscience, and interested students could listen to their presentations.

Some of these guest presentations included topics on alcohol, drugs, and the brain; sex and gender and the brain; and stress, anxiety, and the brain. Not only did this provide enrichment opportunities for students, but it also allowed these college students to get feedback on their approach to teaching (Brown & Hall, 2016). This was a win-win for the high school and the University of Vermont! Before flex time, these presentations would not have been possible in traditional school days.

While looking at another high school's flex time schedule in figure 2.6, one can see there is a 6-day rotation A–F. They have one advisory period followed by two 40-minute flex time blocks. This allows students to schedule time with their mentors during advisory time and build a relationship with their advisory group as a whole. This model once again fits this high school's community, and the model was agreed upon by their staff.

Minutes	A Day	B Day	C Day	D Day	E Day	F Day
80	1	2	1	2	1	2
40	Advisory	Focused Learning	Focused Learning	Advisory	Focused Learning	Focused Learning
60	3	4	3	3	4	3
60	4	5	5	4	5	5
26	Lunch	Lunch	Lunch	Lunch	Lunch	Lunch
60	6	7	6	6	7	6
60	7	8	8	7	8	8

Figure 2.6 One high school's flex time schedule. *Source*: Enriching Students—screenshot.

Step 2: Understand the Structure—Implementation   51

For educators who have not used a flex time model, it is helpful to look at one of the models in figures 2.4, 2.5, and 2.6 and connect it to a familiar schedule. This would serve as a good foundational comparison for a conversation with colleagues about how your school could add flex time into the day. If you are looking at your classes and wondering how to gain more minutes to add flex time, there are a few timeframes to consider: (a) adjust each class to be a few minutes shorter, (b) decrease your school's passing time between blocks/periods by 1 minute, or (c) adjust your homeroom time.

If you are looking at this as a teacher who currently uses flexible scheduling, you may see a model in figures 2.4, 2.5, and 2.6 that you think might fit your school and community better than your current setup. These models might even spark an idea to create a completely original model. The model has to be connected to the wishes and needs of the school community. Remember to always reevaluate your model, as there will be components that work well and others that need improvement. Constant reevaluation as a team will allow your school to enhance its flex time functionality with more precision over time.

Using Flex Time Data to Drive Instruction and Supports

"Rome wasn't built overnight!" This classic statement is one that refers to the notion that success takes time. It does take time, and we are always growing and developing as teams to better support the success of our students. One high school in New Hampshire, in terms of flex time startups, came as close as possible to building their educational "Rome" overnight!

After one semester of using a flex time model similar to the flex time model that another New Hampshire high school uses, this high school saw extraordinary results in the data they collected on the implementation of their block. Very rarely can a school increase academic outcomes, decrease behavior referrals, increase school balance, and produce a model acceptance at a 100% level. Andrew Brauch, a former high school assistant principal in New Hampshire, provided the following results after the first semester of their block in the 2015–2016 school year.

- Total number of A grades increased by 25%.
- Total number of B grades increased by 44%.
- Total number of D grades decreased by 33%.

- Total number of F grades decreased by 41%.
- 97.1% of teachers said the block helps students to be successful in their classes.
- 97.1% of teachers said students turned in more work as a result of the block.
- 70.6% of teachers said students turned in higher quality work as a result of the block.
- 94.1% of teachers said the block is worth the shorter block (81 minutes) compared to the 90-minute block without the block.
- 100% of teachers surveyed said overall the block is a good idea.
- 88.5% of students stated overall the block is a good idea.
- 80.2% of students said the block helps them to be successful in their classes.
- 78.3% of students said the block allows them to keep a better balance between school and other commitments (e.g., sports and work).

We cannot deny the data. These numbers are as powerful as it gets in education. Flex time schools are producing results everyone has been seeking for a long time.

HOW TO COLLECT FLEX TIME DATA AND USE IT TO IMPROVE STUDENT SUCCESS

The following strategies will help you to collect flex time data and then use it to improve student success at your school:

- In your flex time committee, determine what data points are most important to your school (e.g., behaviors, competency/grade outcomes, attendance, student opinions, and teacher opinions).
- Determine how you will collect data—for example, school information system data (e.g., attendance rates from year to year or semester to semester, competency/grade outcomes, and/or discipline reports) and/or student/teacher surveys (remember to refer to individual state laws surrounding student surveys).
- Examples of Likert scale questions for students might include:
  - Do students feel flex time allows them to be more successful in school?
  - Do students get more timely help with flex time than without?
- Examples of Likert scale questions for teachers might include:

Step 2: Understand the Structure—Implementation 53

- ○ Do their students turn in better work with flex time?
- ○ Do teachers feel they can reach more students during flex time than without?
- Examples of open-ended questions for students might include:
  - ○ What do students like about flex time?
  - ○ What could be better with flex time?
- Examples of open-ended questions for teachers might include:
  - ○ What do teachers like about flex time?
  - ○ What could be better with flex time?
- Analyze data as a group.
- Discuss changes (if necessary) to improve flex time for the following school year or semester.
- Send out proposed changes to staff for feedback.
- Implement changes and educate students.
- Continue to do this as your community or school as a whole feels necessary.

THE VALUE OF TIME: A TEACHER'S PERSPECTIVE

In the mid-1990s, the issue of time and how to best use it in high schools became a topic of much interest and debate among educators. The traditional schedule of seven or eight classes ranging from 45 to 50 minutes in length was no longer working for many schools. There were multiple factors that encouraged this feeling, among them the trend toward group-oriented cooperative learning in the classroom.

Teachers were looking to use learning activities that fostered deeper learning and understanding of the curriculum by students, and it seemed obvious we needed more time with students to accomplish this. Serious thought needed to be given to how the schedule could be altered to better accommodate these new approaches. After an evaluation period of almost two years, our school in New Hampshire adopted a block scheduling model beginning in 1997.

Over the course of 15 years of using the block schedule, several surveys showed the staff and students at our school overwhelmingly supported continuing with this schedule—they liked it. Despite the positive feelings, there were problems that needed to be addressed. While the block schedule allowed for greater sustained teaching and learning, teachers still felt the stress of time, students were still underperforming, and failures seemed to occur far too often. At least part of the issue was courses previously running for a full year were now completed in half a school year, so the pressure for teachers to move briskly through their curriculum was an issue.

If Advanced Placement (AP) students needed time to work together to prepare arguments for a debate or a group presentation, it was hard to give up class time to allow them to do so. Often, the process for these worthwhile activities was rushed, and the results were less than what they could have been. Other teachers were feeling pressures, and we were overdue for another evaluation of how to best use our time during the school day.

We looked at all of the versions of the block, but none of them were any better than the 4 × 4 block schedule we were already using. When Brian Pickering walked into a faculty meeting one afternoon in 2013 and said he had a solution to our need for more time with our students, we were all a bit skeptical. However, as a respected member of the community and a former colleague, Brian was a familiar face. He was one of us, which helped him to at least get our attention.

What Brian explained that day made so much sense that we wanted to start it as soon as possible. He called it "flex time," but by any name, our entire staff recognized the exciting possibilities this system presented.[1] By restructuring the schedule to give up just a little bit of classroom time, we could meet with the students we really needed to see, without the distractions of the teacher's lesson, several times a week. Examples of how flex time can benefit students include the aforementioned debate teams who did not have enough time in class for working together to prepare their arguments; students struggling to complete a competency on their own who could get the one-on-one help they needed to complete it successfully; and all the projects we wanted students to complete on time but that needed the guidance and direction of the teacher. These could now be done with quality.

Former high school teacher and social studies department chair, Bill Ranauro, shared the following perspective:

I struggled for years to find adequate time to review and prepare my AP European History class for their exam. With the AP exam beckoning, we always had content left to cover in late April and early May. This was an impossible decision that, as far as I was concerned, had no right answer. If we covered the tail end of the narrative of European history, we would be neglecting our exam preparation; if we spent time in class on exam review and preparation, we were neglecting a portion of the curriculum that would likely show up on the exam.

For years, I was faced with the dilemma of how to best use our time in class. The introduction of flex time helped to solve this problem. I could schedule my AP class for flex time with me several times a week for the several weeks preceding the AP exam. We dedicated that time to exam preparation and regular class time to covering our curriculum. Problem solved!

In addition to all of these possibilities, something unforeseen came about as well. I came to find, when I was busy with one student and another needed me during flex time, many of my best and brightest students were very willing to act as tutors when the need arose. My neediest students benefitted, and, almost serendipitously, I found the system gave my top students an opportunity to demonstrate selflessness and leadership.

All of this was accomplished by scheduling the students who really needed to be with me at the beginning of the week. Sometimes needs change after scheduling has been completed, so it is prudent to develop a system that can accommodate changing needs quickly and efficiently. This flexibility is something that can be built into the system according to whatever the staff agrees to.

Flex time has opened a whole new path for teachers and students to achieve success. Teachers feel a bit less stressed about constraints posed by the limited time they have in class, and students know they can always get the time and help they need from their teacher to achieve academic success. Not every flex time system will look exactly the same, but each school will tailor the system to meet their particular needs. The system is full of exciting possibilities for teachers and students to reach their goals.

FLEX TIME: COLLEGE AND CAREER READINESS

The world is changing! With technology constantly evolving, the workforce is continuing to change also. Some jobs are disappearing, and new jobs are being created daily that require innovation and problem-solving. For our current students, there are jobs that will be needed that we are not yet aware of, which is why critical skills will be far more important than content knowledge.

School counselors are working hard to prepare students to enter this evolving workforce. It is an exciting time, and many school counselors are using software programs to support their efforts in this process. The flex time model is one of the keys to being as thorough as possible with each graduate.

While looking at college and career readiness education in the common historical or basic four-, seven-, or eight-period model, school counselors had to squeeze into classrooms and steal some time away from teachers who are very busy trying to meet their educational requirements. These counselors often have to teach to larger groups to diminish the number of times they have to step into important instructional time. In a time where school counselors are as important, or more important, than ever before, these valuable resources need to be accessible.

Accomplishing this without taking away from the classroom experience requires flex time, which is the answer to solving the ever-challenging logistical concerns of the previous century in secondary schools. It is time to revolutionize this practice and create time for more meaningful college and career readiness education.

In a flexible block or flex time model, students get the choice and opportunity to schedule important school counseling meetings in their instructional day. Rarely will students be pulled out of class for counseling purposes, which for students already struggling in an academic course seems to add to the problem and not diminish the problem. School counselors, on the other hand, do not have to miss out on teaching and the students' learning of important college and career readiness material that further prepares them for postsecondary success. Teachers can even have smaller numbers of students in their sessions to allow for more personalized attention for each student.

School counselors can easily preschedule their students in flex time software specifically designed for the flexible scheduling of students' personalized and ever-changing demands. Once school counselors preschedule students in these sessions, students will get the most out of these sessions using online programs to look into their personality types, career options, personal strengths, college options, and more. This is done in a manner that will help them make more educated decisions on what they may wish to pursue for a career after high school and/or where they may wish to attend college, study at a technical school, or find an apprenticeship. They can do all of this without missing a single minute of instructional time. Of all the various staff roles at a high school, school counselors benefit as much as any role with the variety of different services they can provide for our 21st-century learners.

A school counseling director in the northeast has shown the school counseling world what can be done in flexible time. He and his school counseling team preschedule their students in a sophisticated and strategic manner so that every student participates in a minimum of four small group flex time sessions per year. They do this prescheduling during the summer so all students and staff will know when individuals are scheduled into these sessions.

This allows for no student to be left out of the future growth process anymore. They go through a college/career readiness process with personal strength research, career research, goal setting, and more. The following list includes the school counseling curriculum components that this school counseling department successfully implemented during flex time without any students having to miss class time to do so:

Grade 9: Student Strength Research, Resume Building, Preregistration/Intro to Flexible Pathways, Pop-Up Career Fair, Reflection
Grade 10: Resume Building, Preregistration/Intro to Flexible Pathways, Pop-Up Career Fair, Reflection
Grade 11: Career Research, Resume Building, Postsecondary Planning/Flexible Pathways, Pop-Up Career Fair, Reflection
Grade 12: College (Search, Transcript Request, Common Application), Financial Aid and Scholarships, Graduation, Goal Setting, Resume Building, Interest Inventories, Reflection

This is an extraordinary example of what is possible in the school counseling field with flexible scheduling!

When thinking about readiness for college success, students have to be able to balance their time and meet the demands of their coursework. Flexible scheduling provides students with work completion and time management skills practice in an open-ended yet supported model. Flex time middle and high schools can foster the growth of these valuable life skills over time.

As students enter a flex time middle school or high school, they are instantly given the responsibility of scheduling their flex time to meet the demands of their courses. They have to balance enrichment experiences with extra help. This has a direct correlation with the balance of a college workload and the many opportunities colleges present to students.

Students can begin to find balance in these two accords over time. In a flex time model, middle or high school students are supported in this educational balancing process. Their advisors can verbally work through time management struggles with these students. As students continue to go about this process on a weekly basis, they become better at managing this on their own. This practice has a great rollover effect when these students go to college, because they can manage their time and schoolwork priorities with more confidence and success. As students leave for college and/or the workforce, they take their skills, such as time management, into the next chapters of their lives.

MARENA'S STORY

Marena Brock is a recent University of New Hampshire graduate who experienced flex time in high school and used what she learned to succeed at the next level. She shared this story:

My name is Marena Brock, and I am an alumni of a flex time school. I graduated from the University of New Hampshire's Paul College of Business and Economics with a degree in entrepreneurial studies and a degree in marketing in May 2017. I graduated from high school in June 2013, just 2.5 years after flex time was started. As a student, I was a three-sport athlete, a member of different committees and volunteer groups, had a weekend job, and was overwhelmed and having a difficult time finding the balance between all my different commitments while still enjoying my high school experience.

Before flex time, there was an inconsistency and a difficulty in keeping order and stability. Understanding the hallways of a high school is overwhelming enough as a freshman, but to throw all of the different factors that keep a student well rounded and also expect them to figure out the balance before slipping under academically was a whole different ball game. We had a designated time each week on Mondays called "advisory," which was a time given to homeroom teachers designed to pass out important information and announcements for the week. Unfortunately, this time was not used to the best ability and became a time to socialize with fellow classmates.

The only time to meet with teachers was either before or after school, and if you had theater, sports, or work, or the teacher was unwilling/unable to meet, students were left without the ability to gain the extra help needed to pass confidently. With all these problems, you tend to wonder how others had done it in the past, and why there was no solution to accommodate the issues at hand. But, the system was set in place, and you did the best you could to make the most out of the time you had.

As a sophomore, the reality that academics got significantly harder and more time consuming was a concept that quickly rose into my mind. I was barely passing precalculus, had other Honors courses I was trying to give enough attention to, and had all the other after school commitments I needed to focus on as well. Flex time was quickly implemented after these feelings of sinking started. Understanding what it is and what it was meant for was the first and best thing they could have explained to us. By just giving students 45 minutes during the day to meet with teachers, meet with groups for projects, get homework accomplished, read, and catch up on missed work allowed for such a positive change in my routine.

Initially the concept was hard to grasp—What really was flex time? Giving students broad guidance is something uncommon in the educational system. Rules and regulations are implemented to guide students in the correct direction, preparing them for the future, and teaching them the "correct way" to process things. But, unfortunately, not everyone processes things the same way, at the same speed, and/or in the same environment.

This intervention block gave students the chance to be independent and have the responsibility to choose to prioritize their work and schedule. With that being said, there are always rules carried out to keep order, such as the mindset that the better you did in your courses, the more freedom you had to choose what you wanted to do. Flex time is based on what I would call a "rewards system," which is what kept students accountable. If a student was falling behind in a class and struggled, the teacher, with the student's best interests at hand, had the ability to schedule them in their classroom for part of the week, thus helping the student and giving them the incentive to work hard by rewarding you with the freedom to choose what you would like the better you did in your courses.

The transition was exactly what was expected: students would test the water to see what they could get away with, some teachers were skeptical of the transition, and there needed to be a trial-and-error time to understand what worked and what needed to be modified and altered. What was *difficult to grasp initially was how crucial the trial-and-error time would be to understanding if this was something that could catch on and be as useful as expected, or if it would create tension and more stress. As important and useful as a presentation was on how effective this time could be, firsthand experience really did it justice.*

It did not take long for students and teachers alike to understand how beneficial this time during the day was for them. My grades went up because I had the ability to meet with the teachers I needed to, I was less tired because I was not staying up so late trying to get all my homework done after an away game, and my stress level decreased because there was a safety line thrown to me. There finally was a solution.

When progressing through the years, I used this time to apply to colleges and write college essays that I could discuss with my teachers to ensure I was submitting my absolute best work. There is no specific age or type of student this applies to—it applies to every student at any point in their high school experience. That is what makes this program so unique and applicable in any educational and social environment.

My experience through 4 years in high school was far from boring. It was full, and I was engaged in lots of exciting events that made for fantastic memories. When looking back, I acknowledge how important and how much of an impact it was to have flex time as opposed to those who did not have the chance to experience it. Having the ability to accomplish what I needed to in school opened up opportunities and the ability to have an even fuller experience than I expected.

FLEX TIME: HOW TO CHANGE THE CONCEPT OF "HOMEWORK" TO "PRACTICE"

"Homework." The word students continuously say in agony—and, let's face it, many times parents and guardians as well! As a parent, Brian Pickering sometimes cringes at the idea that, on any given night after a long day for both his daughter and family, they are going to get hit with a grumpy mood around how much homework still needs to be completed before bedtime. There are certain topics that spark interest and strong opinions in education more than others, but it would be easy to guess that none more so than "homework!" On social media platforms, Brian realized if you want to get lots of people sharing passionate opinions in a conversation, just use the word "homework," and your goal will be met.

There likely will never be a time where students will not have assignments to take home, and we are not suggesting students should not be practicing learning goals outside of a school day. But, what if we could balance the way homework is completed and supported for our students? We know that students learn at different rates and that all students need support at different times for different reasons. We know our teachers are doing a better job than ever differentiating their instruction or using UDL to support different learning styles, strengths, and needs.

We now know that, with flex time during the day, students can slow down, extend, enrich, and even present material in different ways for deeper understanding and that homework can be practiced in partnership with the teachers who know them best right in front of them. Teachers can now assure students that they have a concept mastered in a timely manner and help to make their assigned "practice" far less frustrating for the students, parents, and even teachers. We could greatly improve our success in this area.

Of all the survey data collected from teachers since the beginning of flex time, none are more telling than teachers' consistent responses that students produce a higher rate of homework completion with a flex block than without it. Maybe even more importantly, those teachers indicated the "quality of the homework is higher with a flex block than without one." Why? Well, quite simply, much of the homework is not actually completed at "home."

Students are often busier in middle school and high school than they are in adulthood. We continue to pile on these extra hours of homework on students, and they are repeatedly overloading themselves with extracurricular activities. We sometimes forget the value of just being. We do not always allow our children to have down time, be creative, or explore the world around them in a manner that promotes growth and thinking related to their personal passions.

Another strong consideration is the question of what the actual home environment looks like for every child. Is that environment conducive to productive completion of homework? Demands on families to be working second jobs, single parent families, and the pressure for teens to be working or active in the care of younger siblings are higher than ever before.

As educators, do we ever wonder why sometimes homework does not come back to school completed? Do we ever wonder, if it is completed, why it may not be done correctly or with care to support overall learning goals? Even if our students are in home situations that are supportive of the time it takes to complete homework, are our students getting the help they need from their parents when they have questions?

As the demand on teachers increases to cover more and more content to produce higher test scores, we see schools taking steps to add more seat time into their day and remove things, such as recess, at younger and younger ages; and, as students get older, homework levels are only rising. Students spend almost as many hours completing homework as they are sleeping. This can and many times does lead to high levels of stress and anxiety for students and families. As an educational system, we need to find a balance. The flex time model functions as a stress relief system and has been proven to decrease student stress related to completing homework. Student surveys have indicated keeping a better balance between school commitments and extracurricular activities/school work is better with flex time.

While students are in school, flex time allows them to strategically schedule themselves in partnership with their teachers into classrooms where they need to complete homework. They can do this in a manner that is supported by expert teachers who are available to help them get over an obstacle as they reach toward mastery on a specific subject. Before flex time, students would have struggled with a particular topic and would spend time searching for support. It would be "hit or miss" if their time after school or during lunch matched a teacher's time to get the extra help. Can you imagine medical care or medication being "hit or miss" if you needed a doctor? That could be life or death, and while we are not suggesting life or death, we are suggesting academic failure and success can be just as dependent on timely support.

Students may have started by asking their parents for help. In this scenario, many parents would be ill equipped to support their students in completing their work. Let's face it: if a child asked most parents for support in physics, they would be of little help to their child.

This not only wastes time but adds stress to students and many times to parent's lives. As referenced in Bailey's story from earlier in the book, students can struggle to find a time in the near future to meet with a teacher. Getting support would and still often does have to wait days or weeks, which unfortunately widens the learning gap and puts students at risk for falling further behind and potentially failing.

Flex time has removed this barrier and has removed some of the stress homework puts on students and families. Not all students will complete all of their homework at school. Once again, we are not suggesting students should never have some work at home. What we are suggesting is, with flex time, completing homework (practice) in front of the teachers who can help them most will lead to increased academic success for students. We are also suggesting that flex time provides opportunities to balance their days better, knowing there is a period of time where they can get the help they need.

This balance further encourages students to participate in after-school clubs and activities while also giving time to those students who have to work and/or support their families without punishing them for those demands. This flexible time allows students to get help when they are struggling, complete their "practice," and decrease the amount of homework they bring home each day from school.

Also, what if all students had access to other flex time options during this time, such as extensions in art, music, technology, woodworking, foods, and anything else your school provides or would like to provide? Schools could potentially extend their flex time credit/competency recovery options during this additional flex time. They could partner with community members and programs during this time to provide other enrichment opportunities to their students that may not have been possible during the middle of the school day. Students could have more access to ELOs.

When it comes to teacher collaboration time, this extended period of the school day could create more time for teachers to work together in a professional learning community format (Gabrieli & Goldstein, 2008). In a flex time model, these teachers and support staff could schedule staggered days where they could block out their classrooms to meet with their team and better their educational practices as a whole. They could work on interdisciplinary practices with innovative and creative approaches. This is another possible benefit of an extra flex time period.

Flex Time Scheduling Software

The flex time model was something that made sense after the faculty at a high school in New Hampshire spent a year researching, planning, and developing a new system that was ready to roll out. The last problem was: How would a school keep track of students going in different directions in a simple way? This "logistical problem" was and has been the biggest roadblock to schools making such a system work.

From an organizational standpoint, there needed to be a software program that could accurately keep track of the different directions that students were going each day during flex time. Can you imagine using the traditional yellow pass system for teachers in a case where every student in the building was going somewhere different and also finding a way to keep attendance during flex time? It would take the entire 43 minutes just to get students where they need to go—and would they actually get there?

The first attempt to make this work was from a company that produced software for making appointments for doctors at a medical facility. Making appointments for teachers in a system set up for doctors seemed like a possible solution. This failed, as the software, which came from another country, could not handle dozens of teachers loading individual flex time schedules at the same time.

The Internet slowed to a snail's pace, which frustrated teachers and made them question if the school should keep moving forward. Even if we knew this model would benefit students, it was not possible to implement without the technology to support it. This was a true test and a time when flex time could have died before ever getting started.

This critical moment was where teachers could have thrown in the towel—and, quite honestly, who could blame them? This was a system intended to simplify a process to support all students, not one to make it more complicated. The investment and patience during this time made the difference.

Two software code specialists spent several months designing a program specific to education and flex time. They included teacher feedback, and through several iterations and a trial-and-error period, Enriching Students was born and is used today for hundreds of schools across the country. School information systems and other programs have now been developed to support flex time, so now logistics cannot get in the way of this educational best practice.

Step 2: Understand the Structure—Implementation

The software is a critical component to making flex time work. It is imperative that students can be scheduled quickly and that schools can keep track of where the students are during the block. The Enriching Students website includes instructional videos for students, teachers, and administrators to help them learn how to complete different tasks in the program. This has made using the software even easier.

When scheduling students, schools have to preset their teachers, courses, and so on, but, once this is done, the process is quick and easy. As a school, one of the first scheduling questions you will want to answer as a team is: Should we have teacher advisors schedule students or should we have them schedule themselves? There is no perfect answer for this method.

As a school counselor, Nathan Bisson has worked in multiple flex time schools and found out it was easier to have students in his former middle school schedule themselves into their three flex time periods. He learned this was the most time efficient manner for students: to complete this task within one 20-minute flex time scheduling period. However, while working at a previous high school, in a one flex block per day model, it made sense for the advisor to schedule their students one by one during their 43-minute Monday advisory time. This is a decision you will want to discuss as a team.

Once you have made this decision, there will be two scheduling windows that can be used. Let's pretend you decided to schedule students through advisors. After getting into the software and into the scheduling window, a screen will appear with the preset advisory students for each advisor.

There are other software systems that allow you to do this. Some schools have tried using Google Sheets, but that has been too complicated. Some schools use Google Sheets in a different manner to post offerings for a given week for students and staff to see. This is outside of the need for attendance. In terms of the scheduling and attendance purposes, we are most comfortable with this software but it does not mean you cannot find other software to do this in your school.

Once in this scheduling window, there are many ways to schedule students for multiple days at once, but you can view the demo videos on their website to see more of the specifics for this software. Scheduling students in this software has been shown to take 8 seconds to complete, on average, for a student for each day, as Enriching Students supports in their videos. This makes scheduling students to their weekly requests very easy to do. This also makes

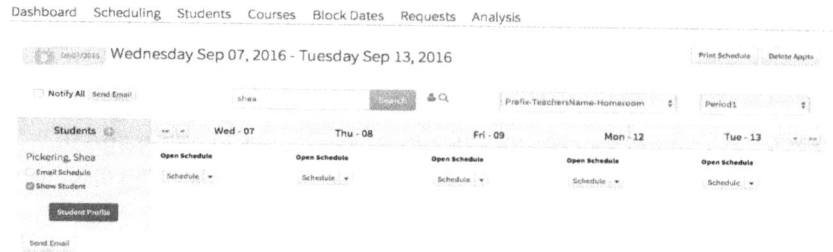

Figure 2.7 Flex time scheduling software example. *Source*: Enriching Students—screenshot.

it easy for teachers, counselors, and other specialists to access the program at any time and preschedule students as needed for any day and time.

The window in figure 2.7 is what every staff member uses to schedule students, even if your staff decides to give students the ability to self-schedule. If students are given the opportunity to self-schedule, their window will look like figure 2.7.

The screen in figure 2.8 is the student dashboard. This is the first window students see when they log into their Enriching Students account. Students can see where they may have been prescheduled by teachers before they click on the Schedule Appointments tab and start picking their flex time appointments for the week. Once they press on the Schedule Appointments tab, they will see the screen in figure 2.8.

While looking at the screen in figure 2.9, students will automatically see teachers with whom they have most recently scheduled. This is a list of their most frequently scheduled teachers, which will allow them to schedule to desired locations faster as they continue to use the software. If students are looking to schedule to a different staff member, they can easily search by department and press "Schedule" on the right-hand side of the teacher's name. Once a student schedules with a teacher, the teacher's line will turn green, and the appointment will be added to their dashboard. This allows the student to see their chosen locations instantly but also allows advisors to see all of their students' course selections in real time in the staff scheduling window.

Overall, whether your school chooses to have staff schedule students or to have students schedule themselves, the students are now in greater control of their education and can build the self-advocating skills needed to succeed in

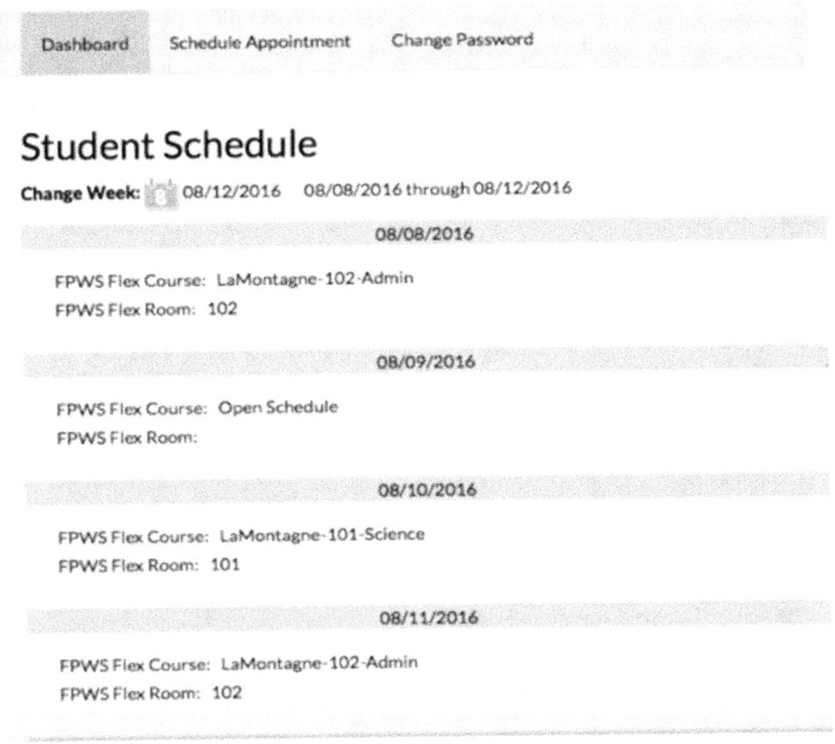

Step 2: Understand the Structure—Implementation 67

| Dashboard | Schedule Appointment | Change Password |

Student Schedule

Change Week: 08/12/2016   08/08/2016 through 08/12/2016

08/08/2016

FPWS Flex Course: LaMontagne-102-Admin
FPWS Flex Room: 102

08/09/2016

FPWS Flex Course: Open Schedule
FPWS Flex Room:

08/10/2016

FPWS Flex Course: LaMontagne-101-Science
FPWS Flex Room: 101

08/11/2016

FPWS Flex Course: LaMontagne-102-Admin
FPWS Flex Room: 102

Figure 2.8 Example of self-scheduling window for the flex time model. *Source*: Enriching Students—screenshot.

the world around them. They now own their time, and that is exciting for all involved. This does not mean teachers lose control, though, as they can look at all of their students' schedules and change their selections as necessary.

Often students will get better at scheduling themselves as the weeks pass by, with teachers working with them to scaffold their time to support their success. Some students who used to need support are making their own decisions to support their success and their passions. Their ability to do what they need to do on their own not only helps them succeed in the four walls of their school but also helps them thrive in the world outside of school.

There are many key features in this software that give staff the ability to help students use their flex time effectively. To name a few, teachers can create special courses for days where they wish to incorporate creative educational practices to support student growth and success. They can repeat flex time options in many different formats: weekly, biweekly, monthly, only on

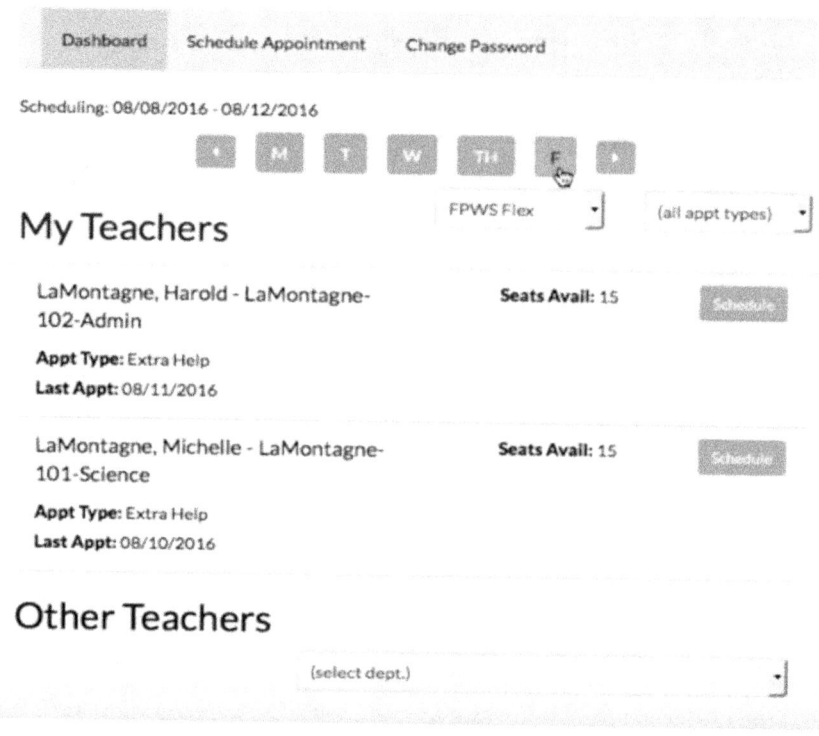

Figure 2.9 Self-schedule software. *Source*: Enriching Students—screenshot.

certain days, and so on. Teachers can block themselves on days they are not available, block the self-scheduling option for students, or schedule multiple students at once.

The type of data this software provides is another feature that supports student success. As a former middle school counselor, Nathan Bisson used this information in the Student Profile section to support student success in parent meetings, child study team meetings, and in the process of building success plans or 504 plans. While looking at figure 2.10, Nathan can see how a student is using their flex time. A few questions to ask while looking at this figure include:

1. Are they spreading out their flex time to correlate with their academic success?
2. Do teachers or advisors need to talk with specific students about how they can manage their time to be more successful?

Step 2: Understand the Structure—Implementation

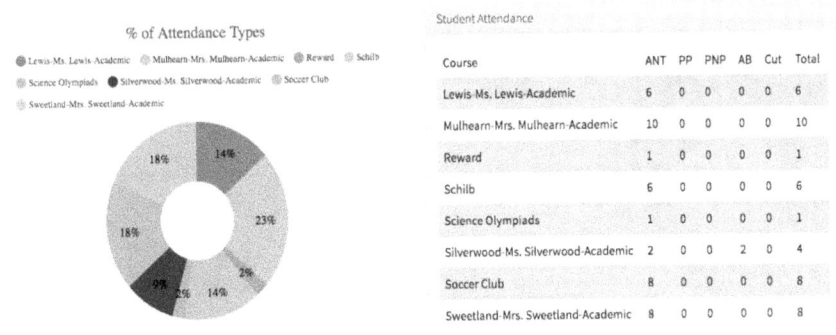

Figure 2.10 **Flex time software—student location report.** *Source*: Enriching Students—screenshot.

3. If a student is struggling in a specific subject, have teachers or advisors scheduled intervention or remediation?

While looking at the pie chart in figure 2.10, one can see this student uses flex time effectively. In this circumstance, Nathan chose to look only at the student's attendance types in their student profile over the past 30 days, but one could go back and look at the whole school year and/or any other time period. This student has gone to sessions in which they needed extra help, such as math, but staff can also see they found time to pursue some clubs they were passionate about, such as soccer club and science olympiads.

In life, we try to use time management skills to create balance in our lives, and this middle school student has scheduled their time in a manner that will be helpful as a skill in high school and in life. They have also scheduled their time in a manner that supports both their academic and mental health. As a school counselor, Nathan sees self-scheduling as another way to build time management skills.

If Nathan was to look at this graph and see an image that showed a student spending 80% of their time in English class, and their grades reflected they were doing great in English but were struggling in math and science, he could bring that up in a brief meeting with the student, as their advisor, to support their time management development. This conversation might also come up in a parent/teacher meeting, where the teacher may decide as a team to preschedule a student into math and science for a period of time to

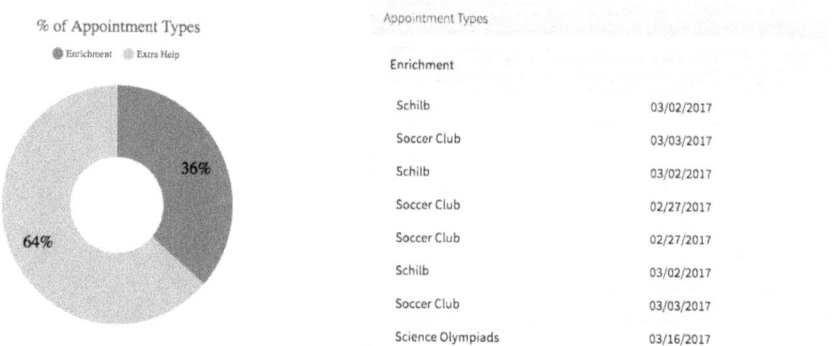

Figure 2.11 Software example for appointment type data report. *Source*: Enriching Students—screenshot.

support their success and the development of positive scheduling habits. If an educator does preschedule a student to a specific location, it is valuable to still have continued conversations with the student on why that decision was made—to support the likelihood the student can take the knowledge gained and schedule time more effectively in the future. Remember, we must help students build these very valuable skills!

While in the Student Profile section, you can also see the percentage of appointment types a student is scheduling or being scheduled to. The student from the previous example has a 30-day percentage of appointment type that can be seen in figure 2.11.

The pie chart in figure 2.11 shows students have balanced their time between extra help in places such as math class and enrichment time in places such as soccer clubs. This student has grades above D and F in all of their classes and therefore does not have any teacher prescheduled remediations shown in this graph. For a student who was receiving remediation over the past 30 days, Nathan would see the third section included in this pie chart.

He can look into each section even further as the right-hand side shows what enrichment options this student was scheduled to and on what days. This is followed by the student's extra help locations (in this program, one can scroll down to see more). This allows Nathan to see scheduling patterns over time. As a school counselor and student advisor, this provides Nathan with the ability to support student conversations with even more specificity.

Every student deserves to be supported, and data are a great way to assist educators in the process of helping students reach their highest potential.

While working with a student who needs a success plan or 504, our team can include data in a plan such as, "Student A should be spending 50% of their flex time in math class." Math teachers in this school can take this information and either preschedule this student into their class for at least half of the available flex time, or they can build a plan where the student schedules themselves and the teacher is checking their profile periodically to make sure this is actually happening.

This student's advisor or school counselor can also support this process in the future, even if they are not attending the school where this plan was originally created. This allows for continued success beyond a student's years in one location. These data and practices give educators the privilege of having knowledge to support all students in a personalized manner as they enter a school rather than students having to figure it out for themselves over time.

NOTE

1. At Fall Mountain, we call this period TEAM time for "Together Everyone Achieves More."

Chapter 3

Step 3: Making it Real—Implementation

Create the Structure, Not the Outcomes

STEPS TO SUCCESS FOR IMPLEMENTATION

As mentioned in previous chapters, any school leader considering implementing the flex time model should begin by noting there are direct connections between the flex time model and SDT. These connections should not be ignored and, in fact, should be used to establish the philosophical foundation and educational basis for the flex time model. Before reading the recommendations for implementation, school leaders should make sure tenets expressed in SDT align with those values in their school.

If a school does not, for example, value autonomy, relatedness, and competency, or does not possess a shared definition of these terms, then the recommendations proposed in this section may not be suitable, sustainable, or practical. Therefore, the first step for any school interested in effectively using the flex time model is to develop a shared common understanding and value of SDT. Once this understanding is shared and expressed, then the entire school (teachers, parents, administrators, staff, and students) can use the characteristics as guidelines for decision making around flex time.

Two of the most often-cited concerns for teachers, when rolling out the flex time model, are the perceived loss of classroom or instructional time and a misunderstanding about what the time should be used for. Unless it is clearly explained, in multiple ways and multiple times, teachers may feel they are being asked to "prep" for an additional class. It is recommended both of these issues be addressed and prepared for prior to implementation. As mentioned earlier in this book, there are important steps to consider when implementing the flex time model. These steps focus on three main themes: (a) building consensus, (b) addressing and discuss potential pitfalls, and (c) gathering a team to observe other schools and bring information back. As one administrator explained in Bastoni's (2019) study:

> I think you've got to start with a team of administrators and find out are we doing this at a district level, are we doing it at a high school only to start? I think it really has to be slowly rolled out so you can find those kinks in your system the first year and then you roll it vertically down. Again, I think it depends on the district and the needs of the kids.

Administrators who have successfully implemented the flex time model also recommend schools interested in implementing the flex time model purposefully focus on the enrichment capabilities of the block. The connection to making up work and improving grades will be obvious to teachers, but other important components of the block may be missed. As another administrator said, "I would say, for schools looking to get into the work now, be very deliberate about embedding that enrichment piece and don't let that fall by the wayside."

When asked about recommendations and advice for schools considering implementing the flex time model, students in Bastoni's (2019) study agreed the flex time model should be implemented. One student said the following: "Do it. Give kids choices, so if they have good grades and they have that choice to have fun." When students were asked what advice they would give to students who knew nothing about the flex time model, but who were going to have it available as an option, they all advised students to make sure they are using their time well (Bastoni, 2019). One student said the following: "I would say take advantage of it as much as you can. . . . Learn how to use your time wisely. And if your work is done, then have fun and do what you want." Another student put it this way:

> Use [flex time] wisely. When you're new here, it's kind of just a thing. It's just there. But when the work starts piling up, it clicks that it's just an opportunity for you to get everything done. They give you a free 40-minute block to just do all your stuff.

Teachers should also be encouraged to get creative with flex time. As mentioned previously, at some schools, clubs like newspaper and yearbook run during the block. Some teachers use the time to write grants, host guest speakers, pilot new classes, or run professional learning communities. The goal should be to make sure teachers know this time can be structured to support their creative ideas and give autonomy to them and students. When asked about advice for those schools interested in implementing the flex time model, one teacher in Bastoni's (2019) study said she thought, if administrators ran flex time, they would form better relationships with students. "I would love to see our administrators also running [flex time] sessions," she said.

This teacher further elaborated on this idea saying, by running flex time, administrators could show students that little piece of themselves in it:

> I don't know, like one of our vice principals loves hockey and if he ran a hockey [flex time block], he would get so many kids there. And I think that would be amazing for him and for the kids.

While this may not be feasible in all schools, her message and the other positive experiences teachers have shared speak to the powerful SDT characteristic of relatedness this block can provide (Bastoni, 2019).

Other practical advice from teachers in Bastoni's (2019) study included paying attention to how many kids could be booked into a room—thirty was seen as too many in one flex time setting by one teacher—and making sure the block was long enough. One teacher said:

> One thing, if I think back to when we first started it, it was roughly 20+ minutes long, and it wasn't long enough. So, they lengthened it. It's like 44 minutes or something now. So, it needs to be long enough, or else it wasn't useful.

Some teachers felt the block should be scheduled at the end of the day, while others preferred having it in the middle of the day so students who had sporting events to attend would not miss it (Bastoni, 2019). Some teachers felt no classes (Honors or other), clubs, or enrichment activities should be held during flex time. For example, one teacher said:

> [I] think whatever you're doing for enrichment needs to be in the classroom, because if it's good enough to do for a little portion of the class, then it's good enough to do for the whole class. Because that might be the one thing that makes that one kid who's not the enriched student want to do better. If you're doing

some cool little enrichment activity, you owe it to the kids who are not interested to try and get them interested.

While most teachers did not agree with this perspective, at least one other teacher did feel offering Honors classes during flex time was problematic (Bastoni, 2019). The goal of the flex time committee should be to ask these questions, attempt to flush out how the majority of the school community feels, and then continuously refine the uses of the flex time model.

Again and again, teachers and students specifically mentioned fun activities or break times as an important outcome of flex time, and many of those interviewed mentioned fun as involving movement or creativity (Bastoni, 2019). One student put it this way: "We don't really have time to let out our energy or do what we want except for lunch. . . . It's nice to get your frustrations out physically or just by drawing. It's nice for me."

Another student said, "I know one of the past teachers . . . he does ultimate frisbee once in a while just to give kids the freedom to just have fun . . . instead of sitting at a desk all day." Teachers also saw flex time as time for students to have fun, likening it to recess. One teacher said, "They want recess, which I wish we had for kids. This provides something like that. An outlet with time for all kinds of activities."

Research and data make it clear students used flex time for different purposes on different days. On some days, in Bastoni's (2019) study, a student used flex time as break time. On other days, they used the time to complete missing homework. In some cases, teachers supported and valued nonacademic activities, such as playing card games or going to the gym; however, in many cases, they did not.

Many teachers and administrators in Bastoni's (2019) study felt students should only be engaged in academic activities during flex time. "This isn't a break. This isn't a time to hang out in the cafeteria. Go to where you need to go," said one teacher explaining how flex time should be used. However, many adults supported flex time as break time or as time to have fun, and some supported nonacademic activities mainly as a reward (e.g., for completed work). Schools interested in implementing the flex time model should be very clear on how the time should/can be used. If they are not clear, then tension can build between teachers, between teachers and students, and between teachers and administrators.

One of the most important recommendations for schools interested in the flex time model is to hold discussions on specific topics prior to implementation. These discussions will not result in total agreement; however, they will allow all voices to be heard, and they will help schools address potential pitfalls ahead of time. For example, leaders who feel break or fun activity time should be allowed during flex time can point to research suggesting break time and exercise, or fun, can actually help students learn.

Break time is especially beneficial for learning in schools using block scheduling. During a class block, students who were given a quiet break, who were told jokes, who listened to music, or who otherwise went "off task" attended to learning at the same or a faster pace than those who continuously stayed on task (Sousa, 2017). In the book, *How the Brain Learns*, Sousa (2017) suggested "teachers are more likely to keep students focused during the lesson segments if they go off task between the segments" (p. 107).

The flex time model positively provides time for breaks or fun activities. One student very clearly articulated the phenomenon Sousa was describing, saying, flex time "gives your brain a break so you can focus more for the rest of the day." Nearly every teacher and all students in Bastoni's (2019) study reported seeing the benefits of break time created by flex time and commented positively on how it provided time for students to engage in movement activities, such as basketball, walks, and games. This idea clearly fits into research showing the brain actually acquires new skills better after exercise. Sousa (2017) wrote:

> The belief here is that aerobic experiences induces greater plasticity in the brain areas responsible for motor skill learning, making it easier for the new motor learning to occur. Here is further evidence of the importance of exercise in school: it can enhance the learning of motor skills as well as cognitive objectives. (p. 109)

Included here are two reflections on the impact of the flex time model. These reflections come from Schuyler Michalak, a freshman at the University of New Hampshire and a Division 1 athlete on the ski team who is majoring in chemical engineering, and from Lily Denehy, a sophomore at Macalester College majoring in history. While neither student mentions SDT specifically, they each shared memories and observations that made clear the connection between SDT and the flex time model.

For example, both Lily and Schuyler reported flex time increased their ability to build relationships with students and teachers. Although in different ways, they also reported how the flex time block increased their feelings of choice or control (autonomy) over how they spent their time. And, despite both being in the top ten for their respective graduating classes, they both said the flex block was essential for homework completion and academic achievement.

SCHUYLER'S STORY

I graduated from high school in 2019. Since graduating, I have had time to reflect on my time there and how it allowed me to succeed in my first year of college as a student-athlete. A major role in my success in high school and proceeding high school was the opportunity the flex time model provided. This time was a very helpful resource that taught me time management, study skills, communication, and self-motivation.

For me, the flex time model was a 45-minute period in the middle of every day that was allotted for individual use. At the beginning of the week, every student would go to their homeroom and book themselves to a teacher from whom they wanted extra help, for whom they needed to make up work, or with whom they needed to get work done. If the teachers wanted to work with specific students, they could also prebook students. Flex time could be used to make up work or tests, get homework done, meet with a teacher, read a book quietly, or work out in the gym.

As a three-season athlete in high school who took multiple AP and Honors courses throughout the school year, I was constantly pressed for time. I would often feel overwhelmed by the amount of schoolwork I had and the little time I felt I had to do it. As someone who struggles with anxiety at times, I would often exaggerate the amount of work I had to do and the little time I had to do it and would therefore become less productive the more I stressed about it. This is where the flex time model really helped me.

It gave me 45 minutes to sit down and either get homework done or schedule out my time in the afternoon around practices and the like. Every Monday, during homeroom, I would spend my time writing down the assignments I had due, what days they were due, when I had practices, and when I could sit down and eat a nice meal with my family. This 45 minutes on

Mondays was an incredible stress reliever to be able to see exactly what I had to do during the upcoming week. I was able to be more productive and use the flex time and my free time to get my assignments done efficiently the rest of the week. This practice I developed in the flex time model carried into my college career.

My first semester I was juggling up to two practices daily with skiing, five classes, and two labs. Applying the skills I learned in the flex time model to my first semester in college allowed me to stay on top of my work. This flexible time also taught me a 45-minute period, although short, can be an extremely productive period. Often in college you will have an hour in between classes, and through the flex time model, I learned how to use that hour most efficiently.

Another way I used the flex time model to help me during high school was to fine tune study skills. On the days I did not have a homework assignment to work on, I would often use the time to study for upcoming tests. Because it is set up so you can go to any teacher, it is extremely useful for planning study sessions with friends and your teachers.

My teachers would often book the entire class and review the material for an upcoming test, or I would book to their classroom to go over confusing material. Having this allotted time with teachers allowed them to teach me a plethora of new study skills to help me succeed in my classes. Learning these study skills has allowed me to perform well in college and taught me how to study productively without the guidance of a teacher.

One of my favorite things about the flexible block was the communication skills I developed in it. During flex time, students have personal, one-on-one time to communicate to your teacher if you need extra help, if you have an upcoming sporting or band event, or if you are going to miss class for some reason. The flex time model taught me the importance of having those one-on-one communications with teachers to be able to succeed in a class.

This time you can spend with a teacher during time that is not structured and therefore can be used for any academic reason. One of my favorite memories from my senior year of high school was getting the opportunity to delve deeper into biology. I was taking AP biology at the time, but I was fascinated by information in the news and current studies going on, and so I would always go to my biology teacher's classroom, and if she wasn't working with another student, I would have the chance to discuss many current events with her, the implications, and the future of science. This really ignited a passion toward biology during my senior year and helped me eventually make the decision to switch majors.

For me, the flexible block provided an incredible opportunity to plan out my time, complete homework assignments, study for tests, get help from teachers, and learn more about subjects I was interested in, but most of all, it taught me self-motivation and standing up for myself academically.

I saw this in other students as well. Flex time not only provided individuals the chance to develop teacher-student relationships and improve their study skills, but it also gave many the opportunity to receive student help. My senior year, I met around once a week with a freshman I had tutored in previous years to help him with his academics. I would sometimes help him with his math, and other times I would just help him organize his schedule so he could excel in his classes. I saw the opportunity the flexible block offered for upperclassman to mentor underclassman as an incredibly positive experience for me and hopefully for him too.

LILY'S STORY

My high school implemented a flex time schedule a few years before I got there. By the time I was a student, it was a well-established program that ran, in my opinion, quite smoothly. At my high school, it was a 45-minute period where students could choose where to "book" themselves to get help, extend their learning, or attend meetings. In high school, I was involved in way too many clubs and sports, was taking too many AP classes, and was working a job. For me, this time was an opportunity to focus on work or classes I may have missed as a result of these commitments during my freshman year.

However, it also became something more for me as the years went on. My sophomore year I joined the student newspaper and literary magazine titled The Link. The Link met during the flex block in the photography teacher's classroom. Our midday meeting time allowed the local newspaper editor to attend and offer us advice on journalistic ethics, design, and methods. It also allowed student journalists the freedom to either work on their articles, schedule interviews, or take photos and work on graphics. This provided busy students like me with a set time, every week, where they could just focus on The Link.

I also began to use this time as an opportunity to work with the Student Leadership Team (SLT). We met once a week as well, and similar to The Link, *it allowed students with commitments after school like sports or work to be part of a leadership opportunity. The SLT developed programming around all sorts of activities, like a dance video to Imagine Dragons' song "On Top of the World" during Spirit Week. Though I eventually left the SLT, it was the perfect group for busy students since all our work could be finished during the flex block time every week and we weren't expected to work on SLT projects outside of that.*

I also enjoyed elements of this time that allowed freedom to work on homework, studying, or to extend learning on a student's own motivation. My last 2 years in high school, I worked on the yearbook, first as staff, then as the editor my senior year. High school yearbooks are a huge amount of work, and afterschool times just don't fully cut it, especially if students play sports, work another job, or have other commitments. The flex block offered the opportunity to work on yearbook pages, photos, and writeups for as many or as few days as needed that week. Some weeks my senior year I booked almost every day to the faculty advisor's classroom while other days I booked 1 or 2 days with her and spent the rest of the time on other work I had.

I loved having the ability to choose how much time I spent working on the book, since some weeks it felt like it was taking over my life, and I would distance myself from it for a few days. Other weeks, such as those leading up to deadlines, I would be grateful for the extra hours I could spend hunched over a computer in Ms. Mitschmyer's room during my school day.

High school students usually have little sway over their day-to-day schedule, but the flex block offered an opportunity to "adult." It was a free space in the day you need to take advantage of—whatever that might mean to you that day. Many days, for me, that was working on extra projects with people from all different parts of the school. Some days, however, I took space for myself and relaxed in the ceramics studio or in the "Zen Den" with one of the school counselors. For me, the most valuable part of the flex block was the trust placed in us as students.

The school was telling us we can make decisions—good decisions—about how to use our time. That gives students confidence. Now, in college, I continue to make decisions about how to spend much of my time. Confidence and time management skills, which were, in part, developed by access to a system like the flex block, allow me to find times to focus and times to relax. That balance is incredibly helpful now and was lifesaving then.

This time was also an opportunity for my school to hold all class meetings for different classes to communicate about current events, college applications, or hold class elections. This was important because the flex block was in the middle of the day, so for students who left school early or came in late because of other commitments, it allowed them to attend without needing to change a schedule at the last minute. Additionally, it allowed many perspectives to be heard on certain issues. Scheduling class meetings when portions of the class cannot be there can disenfranchise those people. Most speeches during elections for student council positions were held during this time so most students could be informed voters.

During senior year, many meetings with important information about graduation, college or job applications, and other deadlines were held during the flex block. Additionally, other opportunities were offered during this time, such as college admissions visits, job/career fairs, and sessions to talk about Naviance (college and career readiness software). Again, these allowed the largest number of students the opportunity to learn about these opportunities.

Another vital high school experience I had with the flex block was the opportunity to prepare, plan, and go on a trip to the Dominican Republic with Ms. Bastoni, the photography teacher, to learn photography techniques and experience another culture. To coordinate the busy schedules of the students who were going on the trip, Ms. Bastoni decided we should meet during this time. Information sessions prior to committing to the trip were held in her room during my freshman year. During these planning stages, Ms. Bastoni also offered us the opportunity for input on a destination and program. We had the freedom to do this because the flex block was not part of a set curriculum, so Ms. Bastoni was not constrained to "teach to a test" or rush through this to talk about the required material.

Instead, interested students had the ability to share their ideas and help plan a trip abroad. I use some of the skills I learned here today. I am in charge of trip planning and coordinating for my college's Outing Club. The organization and openness for input Ms. Bastoni demonstrated during these planning sessions informs how I ask peers at school for input on our long spring break trips. The organization, with lists of due dates and detailed itineraries, is how I structure leader training and the participant application process.

For the Dominican Republic trip, after students had committed and paid the deposit, we met periodically during the flex block to do predeparture activities, meet other students on the trip (since it spanned class years), and discuss our worries and excitement about the trip. I still remember the day Rustic Pathways (the company running the trip) sent out the predeparture boxes—full of information about the trip and the Dominican Republic. That, for me, was when the trip began to feel real. My friend Riley and I were in Ms. Bastoni's flex block homeroom and we delivered all of the boxes to the students who were going on the trip, then spent the rest of the block rifling through our boxes, trying to determine exactly what to expect when we landed in the Dominican Republic. The flex block provided us with a space to expand our classroom learning and plan that expansion with a teacher who was ready to help us do that.

The most memorable and continuing benefit of the flex block, however, was the ability to form relationships with teachers who went beyond just the exchange of school-related knowledge. I talked earlier about Ms. Bastoni, who is still a mentor (or a "frien-tor" as she liked to say) in my life. My last quarter of freshman year, I was in her Introduction to Photography class, and, during this time, I had the opportunity to get involved with the Dominican Republic trip, The Link, and later the yearbook. However, the most important part of all these things was the relationship I built with my teacher.

When my family struggled in high school, I felt comfortable approaching Ms. Bastoni and asking for advice, help, or a shoulder to cry on. For students who may have hard lives at home, building strong relationships with other adults in their lives is vital. The flex block is an important part of this relationship building because it's a time where conversations can flow to subjects outside of the classroom, and there's less pressure to get back on track. Since many students are unaware of resources offered at school, the flex block can be a place to make them aware of those resources.

My senior year, Ms. Goldthwaite helped me schedule an appointment with the school counseling office. My junior year, she and Mr. Bowman used this time to have an informational session about their afterschool ELO class—women's studies. Though the class was offered outside of the flex block, the information session enabled students to learn about it, ask questions, and request time slots outside of school that fit with their schedules. So, they used the time to ensure this class was available to as many people as possible.

Without the relationships I built with Ms. Bastoni, Ms. Mitschmyer, and Ms. Goldthwaite, I would never have been able to access many opportunities and later go to a college that fit my needs and interests.

SUCCESSFUL IMPLEMENTATION OF FLEX TIME IN YOUR SCHOOL

Taking the jump into the flex time model may seem scary. How will teachers react? Will parents support this decision? Will students use the time, or will they wander the hallways? Do not worry. After researching the flex time model, helping implement it in multiple schools, and working/teaching in schools with the flex time model, there are some solid steps educational leaders can take to make the transition smoother.

First, before anything else, those interested in implementing the flex time model should: (a) build consensus, (b) address and discuss potential pitfalls, and (c) gather a team to observe other schools and bring information back. This team should also take point on developing flex time protocols, gather feedback on student and teacher experiences related to the flex time model, and refine the model over time. While there may still be bumps along the way, the following guidelines will help:

1. *Educate your staff on SDT and the flex time model*

    This can be done in many ways. Consider sharing resources, such an article or video. Introduce this evidence at a staff meeting or as part of a professional learning community discussion. Make sure this is structured as a conversation based on the evidence provided.

    Follow up with an email for staff who missed the meeting and include additional resources and a general summary of the discussion. It is recommended you consider sending out a presurvey to gain a better understanding of the current scheduling strengths and needs at the school. Consider sending this presurvey to parents and students as well. A presurvey example can be found in the checklist section at the back of the book.

2. *Determine staff interest*

    After sharing educational materials on SDT and the flex time model, a few times and in a few formats, talk with administrators and department leaders about your idea. Use data from the presurvey to facilitate discussion. Consider asking a small team to visit a school already using the flex time model. Finally, send out a survey to gauge interest in the flex time model and to collect any thoughts, questions, or concerns staff may have. A presurvey example can be found in the checklist section at the back of the book.

3. *Build a flex time committee*

Build a flex time committee based on informal conversations and more formal survey data to determine whether or not to begin the implementation stage. Not everyone needs to agree with the new move, but it will be important to have at least a few strong advocates in all areas of the school, from parents to teachers. Now, create a committee that will work on implementation, creating protocols, managing and setting expectations, and continuous refinement.

This is something that should be open to all staff and students; however, it will be important to have an administrator on this team once it is time to put the final process into action. If possible, this team should visit at least one school using the flex time model. Once the committee is set up, they should work as a group to answer the following questions:

- When do you plan on implementing your new flex time schedule (e.g., next semester or next school year)?
- Have you considered all of the options? What type of flex time schedule will best fit your students' needs? Will you choose to have flex time every day, or will you choose to have flex time on rotating days? There are examples of success with either model. How long will your school's flex time last (e.g., 30 minutes, 43 minutes, or 1 hour)?
- Where will you capture flex time in your current schedule without lengthening your school day (e.g., 6 minutes from each block/period, 3 minutes from lunch, or 1 minute from each passing time)?
- What student management program will you use? Where will you get funds to pay for scheduling software?
- Will students self-schedule, will their teachers schedule them, or a combination of the two?
- What will your school's flex time teachers' expectations or protocols be (e.g., teachers cannot overwrite other teachers in the scheduling window)?

- What flex time options will be available to students (e.g., extra help, interventions/remediations, extensions, or social/emotional supports)? Will your school provide credit recovery options during flex time? Will your school provide ELOs during flex time?
- How will break time and fun fit into the flex time model? What are the best ways for students to spend time during flex time? Does flex time positively impact students who use the time to take a break, engage in movement or creative activities, or simply have fun? If students do benefit from these activities, how can schools support these activities?
- What flex time options will be available to teachers? Will teachers be allowed to hold their professional learning communities during flex time? When will your advisory/homeroom/mentor group meet to schedule? How do you plan on organizing these groups (e.g., eighth-grade survey to group students with a fitting advisor/mentor teacher)? Will they be the same group for 4 years of high school? By grade or by alphabet?

4. *Work together to create a flex time model that fits*

   School leaders should share research on SDT as frequently as possible. This is imperative to building a philosophy that will support the new flex time structure. Consider creating either a new schoolwide vision and/or mission statement to reflect the importance of relationships, autonomy, and competence, or develop a vision statement for the flex time model that reflects these values. For example, a flex time vision statement might read: "Flex time at our school was designed because we believe students learn better when they have choices, build caring relationships, and feel excited about learning."

5. *Create a finalized schedule to present to school staff*

   The committee should design and deliver this presentation. It should include a question period during and after the meeting. This also allows the entire staff to become part of the process of developing the initial plan for flex time implementation. Giving staff and teachers voice when decisions are made is important to promote buy-in and foster a more cohesive school culture. While it may not be realistic for 100% of the staff to believe in any change, having some strong supporters who believe the flex time model is the right choice is important. In many cases, even those with reservations about the flex time model understand the benefits once the implementation was started.

6. *Make adjustments with the flex time committee based on teacher feedback*
   Remember, whatever schedule is set or initial decision is made, it does not have to be permanent. Continue to remind and reassure the school community that this is the initial implementation and there will be periodic surveys and committee meetings to make adjustments and to listen to concerns or suggestions.
7. *Present the education model to your students*
   This could be done in a whole school meeting or in small groups. Make sure you share with students the purpose and vision for the flex time model. It will be important to leave room during the meeting and after for questions and feedback.
8. *Create advisory/mentor groups*
   These are the groups of students that will be assigned to a specific classroom during the school year. At some schools, these groups have remained the same for 4 years, while at others, these groups change each year. As stated previously, grouping can be done through a survey to help match students and mentors by alphabet, grade, or any combination.
9. *Implement the flex time schedule on the planned implementation date*
   The flex time committee should be prepared to meet more frequently during the implementation phase to make small adjustments to your school's model based on teacher and student feedback and to ensure the rollout has a positive flow.
10. *Do not forget to do the following!*
    - Create a flex time committee (if not already created).
    - Survey teachers, students, and/or parents about their thoughts on how to do this at your school.
    - Purchase flex time scheduling software, such as Enriching Students.
    - Create scheduling protocols. For example: do all students with Ds or Fs get prescheduled to the classes in which they are struggling? By when do teachers have to preschedule? Will students schedule themselves or will teachers be the primary schedulers? Will clubs be allowed to run during flex time? Will the school store be opened at this time? If a student forgets a book or an item they need during flex time, will they be allowed to move between classes and how? Will there be special passes?
    - Create opportunities for students to pursue their own passions. Consider having teachers provide lessons on things of interest to them at

this time, such as knitting, yoga, or sign language. This time could be used to extend additional learning or schedule ELOs where students can earn additional credit.
- Determine how teachers can use the flex time model. For example, will teachers meet for professional learning communities during flex time?
- Determine how space will be used during flex time. Will all classrooms spaces, even labs that require safety training like woodworking or automotive, be used for flex time?
- Make sure flex time includes room for mental health or other physical health needs for students. For example, consider offering open school counselor times for students to schedule or bring in outside therapeutic counseling or services during flex time. Some schools use this time to run meditation or Ala-Teen groups.
- Other schools offer parenting classes to pregnant teens or physical therapy for students who receive outside services. Offering these options during flex time means students will not be missing class time or lunch (a key socializing time for teenagers). It can also relieve stress on families struggling to provide these services outside of school hours.
- Provide students with the ability to schedule their flex time for the week on Monday. At first, it is recommended that students be required to work with their mentor/advisory teacher to determine how to use their time for the week. As students mature and learn better time management skills, they can be given more autonomy in this area.
- Create common spaces, such as in the library, where students can schedule themselves to complete work in a quiet space.
- Schedule time for reflection and refinement of the flex time model. This allows schools to continue to add opportunities over time as teachers and students become more familiar with the flex time model.

HOW TO CREATE FLEX TIME PROTOCOLS

Once a flex time committee is established and a schedule is created, it is important committee members create flex time protocols. These protocols are unique to the needs and wishes of every school and how they wish to use flex time. These protocols serve as guidelines to ensure everyone is on the same page when they use flex time. This is an important step because it gives teachers a voice on how flex time will be implemented and ensures staff are functioning as a cohesive unit, so students can function in a consistent flex time model.

This allows students to receive all of the benefits flex time has to offer and can create buy-in for the community. Having a flex time committee create protocols also ensures a school will have teacher advocates promoting and supporting the initiative, thus eliminating the feeling of top-down change so common among educational reform programs. Some examples of flex time protocols are as follows:

- Teachers can preschedule students to their classroom for interventions if they have not met a competency by the end of their course. Teachers cannot preschedule a student to themselves more than twice per week.
- Schools who use letter grades may say teachers can preschedule students for an intervention if they have grades below D, but teachers do not have to wait this long to preschedule these interventions.
- Teacher prescheduling should take place before 10:00 a.m. on Mentor Mondays or any other predetermined scheduling day if there is no school on a given Monday.
- Prescheduled interventions always take priority over student scheduling requests.
- Advisors and other academic teachers cannot override prescheduled interventions.
- Students who miss a Mentor Monday, or any scheduling day, can be prescheduled to their mentor's room for the remainder of the week and can schedule their classes for the remainder of their week with their mentor upon their return to school.

It is important to continuously reevaluate protocols with parents, the flex time committee, teachers, and other school stakeholders to make appropriate edits regularly. This is important because, as the flex time model evolves over time, staff inevitably will find new and creative ways to improve and adjust the use of flex time. Do not hesitate to change and improve protocols. In fact, many schools find a yearly review makes the most sense and allows for continuous improvement and reinvigoration of the flex time model. When reviewing whether protocols are working or not, consider asking the following questions:

- How would your school define flex time?
- What are your school's key components of the flex time model? What is working? What would be missed?
- How and when do scheduling days work? Do teachers feel the scheduling method works?
- How does your school define and implement enrichments, extensions, interventions, and supports?
- What are students allowed to do during flex time in your school?
- What are students' expectations during flex time in your school?
- How are teachers using flex time?
- What do teachers see as the biggest issues with the current structure?
- Are there any misconceptions about flex time that should be addressed (e.g., students are wandering the hallways and some teachers do not have any students booked to their room and use the time as an extra prep)?

Here is a sample of general rules and guidelines for flex time that outline the expectations for scheduling and participation:

- Staff members must check student grades and assignments and schedule students in areas of need.
- Accurate attendance must be taken, and absences should be reported to the flex time advisor.
- Intervention and enrichment opportunities must be provided and should be added to a shared calendar before the scheduling day.
- Students should not be allowed to stay in flex time if they are not scheduled.
- Teachers should make sure all advisory students are scheduled somewhere by the end of the scheduling day. No student should have a blank day in their schedule when scheduling day ends.
- Every effort should be made to sign students up for flex time ahead of time.
- Students may only self-schedule on the scheduling day after their schedule is set, but teachers can reschedule them.

FLEX TIME: SETTING UP AN ADVISORY/MENTOR GROUP

It is our nature not to disappoint the people we care about and especially those who we know care about us. This is true for our students as well. This is why the mentoring role of a student's flex time advisor is ever so valuable. They can give students a reason to push through tough days while helping them build important soft skills that will allow them to thrive in the world around them.

Even though there are many creative ways in which a school can create student groups and pair these groups with scheduling advisors, there are a few methods that have helped our schools to be more strategic in this practice over the years. One example would be to create intermingled grade levels into groups, as this is a valuable way to create lateral student relationships that can promote support and trust with individuals who may not otherwise interact often. These students are at different stages in their development academically, socially, and emotionally. Some students naturally end up acting as peer mentors without even necessarily realizing it. This creates some very authentic interactions among students.

While thinking about creating strong bonds across grade levels, schools can be purposeful in this process. One example of this came from a school teacher committee that created a survey to give to incoming eighth-grade students. This survey connected student interests both in and out of school.

While reviewing these survey results, the staff worked as a team to place these students into advisory groups that brought them together with students who had shared interests. The flex time team also looked to connect students with teachers who had the same passion they did. For example, if there are a group of students who discuss their strong passion for art, the flex time team can connect them with an art teacher as their mentor. This allows the school to preset at least one relationship that can foster mentorship in their most interested areas of education and life.

During this time, students will stay in these groups for 4 years and interact with the same group of students on a weekly basis, given that graduating students will leave and new students will come in every year. In this school, scheduling does not take the whole Monday scheduling advisory block, so students work on their homework in their mentors' rooms some of those days. On other days, teacher mentors will use this time to build soft skills, such as collaboration and grit, in their advisory group through team-building activities. We also use this time for discussion to support our growth as a school through student feedback.

A great example is as follows:

- What is the purpose of a high school education?
- Flex Time Discussion—Lesson Proposal
- *Objective*: to provide a forum for students to share their dispositions and beliefs about the purpose of a high school education.
- *Discussion leaders*: each flex time homeroom will have a designated student leader who will receive training in leading this discussion the week before it takes place. Flex time advisors may choose to join another homeroom if they wish (a mix of age groups, such as a senior/sophomore or junior/freshman pairing, could be particularly effective).
- *Process*
  - 2–5 minutes: while the flex time advisor sets up the media projector and cues to the desired segment of "Losing Ourselves," the discussion leader can open the conversation by asking students the following questions:
    - What is the purpose of a high school education?
    - What did you want to be when you were a little kid? If that has changed, when and why did it change?
  - 10 minutes: view "Losing Ourselves" from 13:47 (Part 4: Worth It?) to 23:00.
  - 20 minutes for this and #4 below: reopen discussion with:
    - Verbalize norms (expectations) for discussion.
    - What comments made by someone in the video clip stuck with you, and why?
    - Questions generated by students/student leaders.
  - Carry on discussion from there, ensuring each student has a chance to speak. If needed, use the following questions to spark or redirect conversation:
    - Why do students go to college? What happens if they don't?
    - Does high school allow students to find themselves/follow their dreams, or does it get in the way?
    - How important is it to get good grades? Do GPAs matter?
    - Should students prioritize getting good grades and high SAT scores or pursuing their own interests?
    - What does success in high school look like?

- One of the debate students says, "People who graduate from high-ranking colleges are more likely to lead happier, more successful, and less stressful lives." Where does this idea come from? How true is it?
- To what extent does the pressure of getting good grades motivate students to learn?
- What do you think Rachel Wolfe wanted to achieve by producing this video? To what extent did she accomplish this?
○ 3 minutes: show the "Most Likely to Succeed Trailer" (running time 2:23) or an alternate clip. Maybe TED talk of Ted Dintersmith's "Prepare Our Kids for Life."
○ 5–10 minutes: continue discussion.
  - For those who saw this documentary, what stood out to you? What questions or ideas did it raise for you?
  - Describe a positive educational experience you have had at your school. What made it positive? Did it involve creating or making something?
  - What would your ideal high school class be like?
  - What is more important to you: learning content/information or learning skills?
○ 2 minutes: exit ticket: tell your advisor one take away (thought, comment, concern) you have from today's discussion.

When comparing this flex time format to one middle school in New England, the style in which they set up their advisory groups is similar, but it is done without a survey. This school is smaller and allowed the staff the opportunity to discuss the best fit more directly in regard to each student. By the time these students reach Grade 6, they have been in this school for 1 year. They are in a primarily self-contained classroom before they start switching classes during the day in Grades 6–8 and start using flex time.

The staff then place students in what they would deem appropriate advisory groups. These groups have shown to be very successful. During the flex time schedule, this middle school has three 20-minute flex time periods per day. This is in a 1-hour sequence right after lunch and recess. Students use the first flex time period on Monday to self-schedule their classes for the week and use the third Wednesday flex time period to work with their advisor to support the growth and development of soft skills, such as problem-solving, collaboration, and creativity.

During this advisory session, students work together on activities teacher/mentors bring to the period. Some teachers have had students compete in blindfolded trust activities, team-building balloon popping activities, and more. While teachers can get creative in their activities during these Wednesday flex time periods, staff work hard as a team to do things that bring students and staff together as a whole school community. Advisories have participated in scarecrow, pumpkin, and door decorating contests—and more. During this time, students grow in their collaboration skills, problem-solving skills, and reasoning skills, which are all so valuable to students.

One group that did not win the scarecrow contest was very excited for the pumpkin decorating contest. With two pumpkins, one was to be in the category of most creative and the other pumpkin was to be the scariest. This group of students was determined to do better. They were given the prompt of what the two categories were.

From that moment, they worked on this project. They discussed who would work on each pumpkin, what design ideas they had for each, and what supplies were needed. It was exciting to sit back and watch this take place, as it felt like they had become a professional team in a matter of minutes.

It could have been assumed, if they were older, that they were part of a graphic design team working on the next Boston Bruins logo or an architecture team building a tall skyscraper. This authentic practice took the mentor out of the equation as the group advisory and made them a bystander who could scaffold thinking as students requested. This mentor was not even needed in the room, and when the students put their pumpkins on display, they were very pleased with their products and their valiant efforts.

Whether talking about advisory groups at the middle or high school level, it is important to consider how you, as a school, wish to interweave students into advisories and how to pair them with a teacher. There is no method considered better than the other, but the model and functionality of this process has to fit your community and the needs and growing passions of your student body. Teacher mentors and their practices during this time can help the school culture tremendously at both the middle and high school level, as we see this time with students as a soft skill building center for success.

HOW TO SUPPORT SELF-DETERMINATION THROUGH THE FLEX TIME MODEL

Autonomy

The flex time model empowers students to take ownership of their learning. In the traditional schedule, students attend four, seven, or eight classes per day with no deviation and no control. They have no extra time in the day to work with their teachers to gain academic support through relearning, more individualized instruction, support from peers, and/or enrichment, unless they get lucky with after-school time that matched their teacher's schedule.

Using the flex time model, students can work with their teachers to map out how they will use the time and thus develop time management skills and increase their feelings of autonomy and choice. The flex time model allows for more timely support during the day and helps students balance commitments after school. It even allows schools to rethink the concept of homework because of the time during the school day flex time provides.

While the flex time model empowers students, it should be seen as a partnership with teachers. With this model, if students fall behind or do poorly on assessments, teachers can immediately schedule them to meet during their flex time. Teachers often preschedule students to their room if they are struggling or missing assignments for the upcoming week. Students see this on their scheduling portal when they go to schedule on Mondays during their scheduling advisory period. This often pushes them to get their work done so they can free up their flex time in future weeks.

Students have an incentive to be successful so that they can use this time for their own balance of academic needs and interests, but with the understanding that the teacher's mission is for them to succeed academically, so they will take charge when needed. Students are often prescheduled to those specific classes where they are struggling, and they know through well-communicated flex time expectations that their classroom teachers will preschedule them. This incentive has improved learning for students in flex time schools by using this collaborative student and teacher partnership through clearly articulated expectations. This formula creates a level of motivation that layers on top of a student's intrinsic motivation to excel.

While creating this on-demand educational model, students are more in control of their learning than ever before. Not only is this strategic block set up differently for every student's needs, it is much more than that. No longer do students need to carve out time before school, during lunch, or after school to get a little help from specific teachers. We all know this process could take a week or more at times to connect with a staff member, and, by that point, the student has already fallen too far behind to stay on pace with the rest of the class. We like to compare this timely support (or lack thereof) with the medical field.

When someone is ill, it is critical they get treated as soon as possible. Early detection in the medical field is most important to stay healthy, which is quite obvious to all of us. Education is no different. When we experience a learning gap and fall behind academically, we need timely support so we do not fall further behind. With flex time, students get the differentiated support they need in the moment and move forward with the rest of the group, which gives teachers a new way to facilitate a more functional UDL.

When it comes to personalized learning through flex time, students can take their education to a whole new level in a manner that supports their individual passions. The flex time model engages students and creates enthusiasm for students at a much higher level. Let's think about the average student who does well in every class but still finds school boring. What if every day they could spend more time in a classroom that specifically connects with their interests, or if they could take an assignment or task they enjoy to a higher level? In a student survey conducted in 2016 at a New Hampshire high school, students shared what they gained through flex time was "making progress towards deeper learning."

If a student has a passion for art, they could work on an extra project with the support of their art teacher, and the project could be another piece in their portfolio, but through the intrinsic value to the student and not the extrinsic value of "I have to do this for the grade or my transcript." Grades and transcripts will take care of themselves when students and teachers create this culture and personalize learning. A student who loves graphic design could work with the school newspaper and design their typography to take this club to another level. A student who loves science could take an extra online course in a subject their school does not offer.

If a student loves music, they could work with other music students during flex time to compose an original piece of music. If a student loves being in their automotive class, they could spend that time with their teacher learning how to change a car's transmission with more confidence as more time has been spent on the skill. Students at this high school also stated flex time allows them to "make progress towards deeper learning."

When it comes to students and personalized education, students can, and more often times will, experience a higher level of engagement and achieve more, not because they have to but for the love for learning. Guy Donnelly, a high school principal in New Hampshire, supported the notion that flex time positively changed the culture and did so very quickly. Six years ago, their school's attendance data were at 89%, but, after a year of flex time, the student attendance rate increased to 93%, which is above the national average. This data point, along with several other indicators, clearly indicated that these students had embraced the flex time model.

It is easy to see how any student who has a passion can personalize their education and decide how they want to spend their flex time. Flex time creates time and opportunities for students to find a passion or talent they may not know even existed. Let's face it, having a specific path or direction or knowing what their future career might look like as a sixteen-year-old is not the norm.

As Anschuetz (2015) wrote in *USA Today*, citing data from the National Center for Education Statistics, roughly 80% of students change their majors before they graduate. Thus, do we really expect or even know what a sixteen-year-old will do when they are thirty? As we have said, the flex time model puts students at the center of their learning and in collaboration with teachers who know them best, thus creating an atmosphere where students love to be.

HOW TO SUPPORT AUTONOMY THROUGH THE FLEX TIME MODEL

The following recommendations can help you to support the autonomy of your students through the flex time model:

- Create a flex time committee (if not already created).
- Survey teachers, students, and/or parents about their thoughts on how to do this in your school. Purchase flex time scheduling software such as Enriching Students scheduling software.
- Create scheduling protocols: do all D/F students get prescheduled? By

when do teachers have to preschedule? Are students going to schedule themselves or are teachers going to be the schedulers?
- Create opportunities for students to pursue their own passions during flex time (this could be through extensions such as ELOs).
- Create a flex time system that allows students to take care of mental health needs (e.g., opening school counselor times for students to schedule to or bringing in outside counselors to provide therapeutic counseling during flex time). This can relieve families of the stress of getting students to counseling outside of school hours.
- Provide students with the ability to schedule flex time on Mondays for the week with teachers to get extra help from teachers as needed.
- Create a learning commons, such as in the library, where students can schedule themselves to complete work in a quiet space. This can help to reduce homework amounts and ultimately reduce stress after school.
- Add flex time opportunities over time that allow your students to develop their passions and increase their excitement to go to school.

Competence

Teachers learning to use UDL have become more common, and this philosophy certainly supports the belief that all students have different learning styles, strengths, challenges, and rates of learning. Since students have different strengths and needs, the planning and execution of lessons for all students can seem daunting to teachers. UDL is also great for parents and students who struggle with the idea that their student may be able to move faster and extend their learning and believe that they should not be held back in a heterogeneously grouped course. UDL can help with this issue. So, how does flex time simplify and maximize this common concern? Here is a real-world example with the potential of solving this through flex time.

A high school in New Hampshire had "leveled" a general and Honors freshman physical science course for many years. Carol Young, a talented and experienced teacher, was willing to think outside of the box and tackled this problem by combining the two levels into one heterogeneously grouped course but with a plan to use flex time to extend learning. She took the two classes of freshman science and gave all students (and their parents) 3 weeks to decide if they wanted to "extend" their course work for Honors credit.

Carol offered the core curriculum to all students during their regularly scheduled class time. She shared with all students and parents that if any student wanted to take advantage of the Honors credit (and, more importantly, extended learning), they would need to show competency in the school's "self-management" 21st-century skills rubric in the first 3 weeks and have the desire to use one flex time block a week (Thursdays) to engage in this learning. Of the approximately forty students, twenty-three of them chose this option and started their journey in the fourth week of the semester.

Carol then designed a performance assessment project to be built around a specific interest for each student that would include science concepts and a mix of the school's identified 21st-century skills. These twenty-three students worked all semester to create their own invention based on research and in collaboration with at least one community member who had expertise on their chosen topic. Carol met with them every Thursday during flex time to provide formative feedback and support. She also made sure they were moving forward each week with goals established to meet their timeline.

For the seventeen students who chose not to extend to the Honors option, they were scheduled for the support needed to meet the core curriculum, and the results were very positive for all involved. Carol offered performance presentations at the end of the semester for her twenty-three students, and they presented their projects in front of parents, the community, and staff members. UDL, to match students' passions, strengths, and needs, was maximized through the use of flex time.

Another important point to consider is the flexibility that Carol had to be creative and explore as a teacher. As principal, Brian Pickering did not tell her she had to do this; rather, it was her own idea, as she knew she had the support to simply "try." The result was a successful presentation at a faculty meeting and a dialogue among teachers on how they could implement this type of opportunity in their own classes. We learned, over time, the best professional development for our staff is when teachers shared their experiences with others.

Most faculties have their own experts in certain areas, and building a professional learning committee where teachers share results, practices, successes, and even failures can lead to improved learning and continuous growth. As we rethink the way we structure our educational day, we can create opportunities in flex time to enhance best practices in the RTI arena.

Teachers and specialists can meet the immediate need of these students quickly and efficiently and, when necessary, can take control of their students' flexible schedule to help them get their education on track.

Relatedness

"Does Johnny need to be in class, or does he need to see his school counselor?" It is an unfair battle for both the teacher and the school counselor to try to determine if academic or socioemotional needs are more important than the other. This is a lose-lose situation. Both of these professionals want to provide their students with the tools they need to succeed.

As a school counselor, flex time blocks have dramatically changed the way we practice in schools today. No longer do we have to struggle with the historical battle of trying to explain to a teacher why we need to see Johnny. We know both academics and socioemotional needs are important!

The answer to this dilemma is easy with flex time. School counselors can schedule students they need to see during the school week for noncrisis counseling without having a student miss a minute of instructional time. Isn't that exciting!? It doesn't stop there! School counselors can run small groups during this time.

They can provide groups such as resiliency groups, anger management groups, social groups, and more. A high school in New Hampshire even has a Zen Den during their flex time focused on mindfulness practices. This flex time for counselors can be personalized to improve learning for all students, and it can be adapted to the needs of a specific school, counseling team, and, most importantly, students.

We all know the growing need for counseling in schools, and flex time allows these school counselors/student assistance counselors to see students without having them miss any class time. We all know that there are many students who should have the best of both of these worlds. The answer is now in flex time. Some schools take flex time a step further and use community partnerships with outside counselors to provide further mental health counseling to students who would not have access to counseling outside of school because of a variety of obstacles (e.g., lack of transportation). With our national issue surrounding high numbers of drug abuse and addiction among students, schools can now provide extended individual counseling, support, and even education to individual students or groups to support the success of these students in the most effective manner possible.

Some schools even have clubs for their students during flex time to support students' mental health. Students in Grades 6–8 can be seen at a New Hampshire elementary school taking time to enjoy clubs, such as weight lifting, chess, science olympiads, newspaper, soccer, recycling, and more, that give them a break from the normal grind of school work. While students participate in activities valuable to their mental health, they learn work-life balance. As adults, we continue to work on this on a daily basis as well. These are a few local examples of mental health options for students created in a flex time model.

While students in our nation continue to struggle with mental health, they may be so busy with school work that they feel they cannot afford to miss class to meet with a counselor. Early support is ever so important, with supporting mental health. By having flex time, students can visit counselors without having to miss even a minute of class.

As previously stated, group counseling sessions such as boys' groups, girls' groups, resiliency groups, substance abuse support groups, and more are often available to students during this time in many schools. All of this combines to support the mental health of students. Flex time for counselors limits the conflict of working with students during their academic class time while still addressing their most critical social and emotional needs in a timely manner.

Over the course of one semester of flex usage at another high school, in 2010, students reported their stress and anxiety at school decreased a total of 6.4%. This, at the midway point in the semester, had dropped 3% (Pottage & Sillery, 2016). Over time, it can be assumed this percentage of stress and anxiety in this school would continue to decrease as students become better at using their flex time more effectively based on their individual needs.

Students at this high school are choosing between different flex time options such as completing homework, socializing with friends, getting academic support from specific teachers, participating in wellness activities (e.g., yoga and going to the gym), and other activities (Pottage & Sillery, 2016). Students are building time management skills and engaging in wellness activities during this time. The ability to balance these dynamics is so valuable in the world outside of high school. The practicality of flex time is a chance for students to truly take care of themselves. On some weeks, students may need to use all of this time to complete their coursework, while other times they may need to take a mental health break and participate in wellness activities or seek counseling.

No longer do we have to make these decisions for our students, but rather we can let students learn how to control their education during this time. Mentally and physically healthy students who balance academic, social, and emotional support contribute to a strong school culture that can help all students succeed. Flex time sets the foundation for this by giving students agency to determine what they need and when.

At all flex time schools, students may wish to take a mental health break from their daily academic grind or to make sure all of their work is up to date. Some examples of wellness activities include attending a flex time session, like their high school's Zen Den, where one of the high school counselors facilitates mindfulness activities for students. This is a very popular group at one flex time school, and students love attending these sessions. The counselors are not only giving students a space to take a mental break, but they are giving them skills to support their mental well-being throughout their lives. A former parent of a New Hampshire high school student stated:

> There is no doubt in my mind your institution of flex time is one of the reasons why [my student] enjoyed success while at [his high school]. It gave him the individual attention he needed, *when* he needed it. flex time made his time at school so much more productive and relieved some of the stress. It enabled him to go on to even greater stress at the University of Massachusetts at Dartmouth!

In regard to the mental health of our school teachers, flex time gives them time to facilitate clubs and ELOs that connect to their passions and increase their overall well-being. Teachers can help students get caught up during the school day rather than spending more time after-school working with students in this capacity. They can finally connect with their educational peers during the school day to collaborate and build the interdisciplinary lesson they had wanted to do but never got around to completing. Students' mental health is important, but all too often we forget teachers' mental health is important too!

Learning environments that benefit students and allow them to be creative with their interventions and extensions will offer a refreshing change to their otherwise very structured day. By allowing teachers to have the time to have this ownership, schools are increasing teacher autonomy. Districts can and should view this time as an investment, not only for students and their success but also for teachers. Teachers who are mentally well and enjoy their work day will take fewer days off from work and cost the district less money when they do not have to pay substitutes to be at school. This flex time also alleviates the pressure for teachers with after-school help and allows them to better balance their own lives (Pottage & Sillery, 2016).

HOW TO SUPPORT RELATEDNESS THROUGH THE FLEX TIME MODEL

The following recommendations can help you to support relatedness through the flex time model:

- Discuss social/emotional support options with your flex time team/committee.
- Survey staff in this area, such as school counselors, student assistance counselors, social workers, and local mental health providers on how they could support students' mental health needs through the use of flex time.
- Create flex time opportunities in the flex time software that students can request to sign up for. Examples include:
  - Student assistance counselors could have open windows for students to schedule on an as-needed basis. They could also preschedule students in small group counseling sessions during flex time.
  - Mental health counselors could preschedule weekly counseling sessions for their students in the flex time software.
  - School counselors could open their flex time once a week for support sessions.

Remember, all of these supports can happen without students missing any class time, which can often be a reason why students do not seek mental health support. They no longer have to choose between academics and their mental health. They are both important!

RESPONSE TO INTERVENTION AND THE FLEX TIME MODEL

RTI in its best form happens in flex time. Just like a car, you want to schedule preventative care and make sure the car has everything it needs to run smoothly. In school, preventative maintenance is Level 1 RTI where whole classroom lessons allow students to build skills teachers think will help them thrive.

Similar to car maintenance, sometimes you do everything you can to prevent the vehicle from breaking down, but things end up not working the way they are supposed to. We could schedule an appointment for this little issue with our local mechanic for 3 weeks later when they have an available appointment, or we could find someone to take our car the same day to get it on the road right away. What if education had a same-day service always available for every student who did not get everything they needed in their Level 1 RTI whole classroom lesson?

Daily flex time is the biggest step for all students in secondary education, a step taken to accomplish the goal of "keeping your car on the road" and not in the shop. The well-researched theory of RTI is broken up into three levels of support. Level 1 is the day-to-day interventions that may be needed and are available to all students, usually directly with their classroom teacher. Level 2 is defined as a student needing additional support, which may include the intervention of another adult or supports beyond day-to-day interventions. Beyond the classroom, 88% of students at a New Hampshire high school indicated that one or two flex time sessions per week are enough to get them caught up and help them to better understand the material.

Level 3 is defined as students needing more significant support, which means a specific individualized education plan (IEP) and the support of a staff specialist. Level 2 RTI does not have to wait for specialists to have the time to pull students from class time. Teachers can preschedule these students based on conversations with them, other teachers, or after looking at their grades/ competencies. They can give students the quick fix they need, or they can connect students with a specialist during that time for the next few days to help them get back on track. This could include a math or writing tutor and/ or a reading specialist.

Without this flex time to meet the immediate needs of students, we would see students fall further and further behind as they have not been able to engage in reteaching to catch up to their peers and would fall further behind over time. As educators, we want to create the best educational model for high-quality learning, and flex time allows us to do that efficiently and effectively in the world of RTI. At this New Hampshire high school, students' number one reason for personalizing their learning during flex time was "taking advantage of individualized help in subject areas."

When it comes to Level 3 RTI, we have to continue to use quality interventions to support student learning. This may include only a fraction of our students, but it can be supported effectively during flex time. Students can work in a supported flex time with specialists available in small teacher-to-student ratios. This time is often prescheduled for students through a 504 or IEP, and it gives students the direct support they need in an environment with more than just one teacher in the classroom.

Other examples of Level 3 RTI include any other special education services that would normally happen during the school day and would cause students to be pulled from classrooms. In the flex time model, specialists could work with students and maximize the least restrictive environment philosophy we know benefits all students. Flex time can be run as a fully inclusionary time and can limit the need to remove students from their classes for specialized instruction.

The partnership from [teacher] with our family for my daughter has literally saved her academic life! I realize it's a 504 plan support, but the fact remains, with [teacher]'s support, love and partnership, our daughter is now focused on her future and working more independently towards her goals and she is currently a straight A student.

We moved here a couple of years ago and could not be happier with the school district here! Our old school district never offered anything like (flex time)—it is a wonderful opportunity for the students to get extra help when needed and we are also pleased that if they are doing well in school they have the opportunity and responsibility to make their own choices for how to spend their [flex time] time. Wonderful, innovative program!

- 86% of students agreed, "Flex time allowed me to improve my learning."
- 88% of students agreed, "One/two sessions are enough to get me caught up."
- 81% of students agree they "took advantage of enrichment opportunity or extended learning opportunity."

HOW TO SUPPORT RESPONSE TO INTERVENTION THROUGH THE USE OF FLEX TIME

The following recommendations can help you to support RTI through the use of flex time:

- Discuss RTI through flex time with your school flex time committee.
- Survey your school's specialist to see how they would like to use flex time to support RTI (e.g., reading specialist prescheduling students for RTI Tier 2 and Tier 3 supports during flex time).
- Create session student limits to prevent extra help sessions from being over crowded (e.g., twelve student maximums in sessions that are not custom session creations).
- Offer competency recovery/credit recovery flex time options for students, which eliminate the need for them to redo whole courses when they fail. This can support them in getting the help they need and moving forward. You may have one teacher in each department designated to support these recovery options during flex time.
- Allow teachers to be creative in the way they offer RTIs for their students during flex time. This could be done in a collaborative effort between school staff members.

HOW FLEX TIME BENEFITS EXTENDED LEARNING OPPORTUNITIES

Tell me and I forget, teach me and I may remember, involve me and I learn.

—Ben Franklin

Mary Lou O'Neil provided us with a wonderful perspective on how to best support ELOs through flex time.

Each student learns differently. As we move toward more personalized learning, having a variety of educational options for each student is crucial. The manner of learning and the setting can be important and different for each student. Some students do well in traditional classrooms, and some students do better by learning "outside of the box." Having more ways to learn—and places and times to do it—can be an important part of every student's education and the key to learning for many who have struggled to learn in the past.

Simply put, without flex time, all sorts of ELOs would be made more difficult, if not impossible. Extended learning opportunities can include internships, job shadows, company tours, work-based learning, performing groups, sports teams, and co-ops, and they can be combined with traditional classes, as well as individual and group ELOs. All types of ELOs are made much easier with flex time in the schedule. You may be more familiar with internships—the opportunity for students to test drive potential careers by working with a local business.

Extended learning opportunities include internships, but they are more broadly defined as a credit-based learning experience that takes place outside the traditional classroom. It is an individualized learning experience created by the student, a teacher, and a community partner and is intentionally designed to be a school/community collaboration, driven by a student's interests, that can be flexible in time and place. Extended learning opportunities are one more way schools are making learning more relevant for more students. Managing school schedules to allow more students to use the community as a classroom, and allowing more community and business partners to come into the classroom, is part of an inexorable shift in how we educate students.

BACKGROUND ON SEAT TIME VS. FLEX TIME

The following contribution is from an interview with Fred Bramante, a long-time educational reform advocate and a former chair of the New Hampshire School Board:

For over 100 years, schools awarded credits based on the number of hours students were in school—or in their seats, also known as "seat time." What students earned for grades, or what they learned didn't matter! As long as they were awarded at least a D for a grade, they received the same credit as a student who received an A.

Allotting "Carnegie" units/credits based on seat time started in 1906 at a conference at Harvard University. Educators were trying to find a standard for providing benefits to college professors. They decided full-time professors deserved benefits. The definition of what full-time is became formalized as 180 days.

If you taught for 180 days, then you were a full-time professor and therefore entitled to benefits. High schools adopted, basically, the same model and decided if students were in school for 180 days or 120–150 hours of classroom time, they would be awarded a Carnegie credit. New Hampshire chose 135 hours as the standard for credit (180 days × 45 minute classes = 135 hours). If students earned Cs and Ds, but satisfactorily completed the hours, they moved on.

Eventually, in 2005, the New Hampshire State Board of Education, headed by Fred Bramante, determined seat time was not a good measure of student learning. Why 180 days? Was there any research that said 180 days was important to learning? The answer was "No." Mastery of Competencies became the new standard. Schools were charged to offer the same number of hours (990) no matter how they decided to plan their calendar (5.5 hours/day × 180 days = 990 hours or 6 hours/day × 165 days = 990 hours), but they were no longer required to do 180 days per year.

At the same time, the New Hampshire Department of Education questioned how credits were awarded. If you showed up for PE class, you got a PE credit. If you were on a sports team, worked strenuously, and were likely more fit—no credit. The NH Department of Education asked, "What if the exact skills could be learned outside of school, should that count?" The board decided "Yes." Where else could students learn? At an auto dealership, a space camp, or through travel? If skills and competencies are demonstrated, the answer should be yes.

What if three out of four competencies are learned, should that be okay? The board said "No." Students are required to "master all required competencies." Fred gave this example: if you are learning to fly a plane and you get an "A" in takeoff skills, and an "A" in keeping the plane in the air, but get an "F" in landing . . . that's not a C. There should be no credit until all required competencies are mastered!

The goal in 2005 was to eventually have a personal education plan for each student and be able to provide a customizable education. Fred noted progress had been slow. He also noted, to provide a customized education, you cannot really do that within the walls of the school and a traditional school day schedule.

In 2005, New Hampshire was rethinking the notion of school schedules and where/how learning takes place. This was the beginning of including ELOs for school credit.

HOW FLEX TIME HELPS MAKE SCHOOL/ BUSINESS PARTNERSHIPS POSSIBLE

Mary Lou O'Neil was an internship coordinator for an NH high school. She was an amazing asset to connect school and community. She was recognized for her outstanding work preparing students with work place skills. Mary shared the following perspective on the value of flex time in the success of her role.

For 20 years, until I retired in 2017, I was the school-to-career/ELO coordinator at a high school in New Hampshire. My goal was to find "a happy match" for students—an internship where they could set personalized learning objectives and learn about potential future careers. My role was to help students do some self and career exploration activities that would lead to a work-based learning internship.

I held workshops to help students think about the various careers that might be a good fit for their interests, abilities, and job values. Once we defined those filters, and identified their Holland Code work personality type, we could find several jobs that were likely to be a good internship fit. I would reach out to businesses that most closely matched a student's career interest.

Fortunately, many businesses are eager to partner with schools—not only to help individual students but also to help train the future workforce. In a relatively rural community spread over nine towns (and over 20 years), well over 300 sites said "yes" when asked to mentor a student intern. Given the rural nature of our area, having enough time to travel to and be at the site—roughly 7 hours per week—made having flex time in each student's schedule very helpful. On average, about 40 students per quarter took a 90-minute elective internship block.

Sometimes we found placements within the school setting, but more often it was done at various businesses throughout the community. At my high school, we had a 40-minute flex time, 5 days a week that added a time cushion for many of those work-based internships. That 40 minutes of flex time also created the opportunity for community people to come into the school and talk to students about their careers.

IMPACT OF FLEX TIME ON STUDENT SUCCESS AND ITS VALUE TO THE BUSINESS COMMUNITY

I love when a happy match sparks a vocational interest for a student. Knowing what the "piece of cheese" was they were working toward, I could see heightened interest in further learning. It helped some students stay in school rather than graduating or leaving school early. For others, their ELO was an exciting learning experience that gave them the chance to step outside the typical student role and work with an adult mentor in a way that was different than working with a teacher. One of the most rewarding parts of my job, and I have heard this from other ELO teachers, is seeing the growth in maturity and confidence ELO students show after successfully navigating the uncharted waters of working with new adults. Sometimes it is even fun!

One site supervisor told me a mother of a student at his bakery came in to thank him. Her daughter was not excited by school, but her internship made her happy and was something she really looked forward to. The baker taught the student how to make dog biscuits, and they sold them in the bakery as "Emily's Bow Wow Biscuits." The local paper published a picture of Emily feeding her Bow Wow biscuits to the site supervisor's two dogs—a delight for all involved!

The value of seeing the working environment, experiencing workplace expectations, and meeting people in the field—as well as learning about the different jobs and skills needed for those jobs—is an "aha" moment for many students. Suddenly they can see themselves in one of those jobs doing road and infrastructure repair with the Department of Transportation or opening up their own bakery instead of going into the family's hair styling business. Or perhaps they see themselves pursuing further training to enter a field they may have never considered before—a metallurgy engineer in advanced manufacturing—or choosing a specialty from a wide range of health-care careers—medical assistant, audiologist, radiologist, prosthetist, naturopath, veterinarian, etc.

I particularly like seeing former interns who are now successfully working in local businesses. There are students who work at, or who own, a car repair shop; interns who have "graduated" to police officers in surrounding towns; the medical assistant in the local hospital's pediatric office; or the vet tech at the animal care clinic where I take my cat. What a bonus it is that these young people have chosen to "stay, work, and play" in our community.

Not only do ELOs benefit students, but the importance to the community of creating business/education partnerships is no small thing. Ideally, these partnerships can be a win/win situation where a student receives valuable training while test driving a particular career—and sometimes employers are test driving potential employees as well. Students can end up as local employees—or even employers.

Perhaps most important is that stronger relationships are built between schools and the community. This is huge and can be helpful in so many ways. If local businesses feel the schools are aware of their training needs and are helping with local workforce development challenges, then a beautiful relationship can start—as well as an important and mutually beneficial partnership. Companies have donated equipment to New Hampshire schools, have come in to do mock interviews with students, and overall, appreciate being involved with the schools and the students in their community. Being flexible with where and when learning occurs may also mean students can do a summer internship, which can sometimes lead to a future job.

IMPACT OF FLEX TIME AND EXTENDED LEARNING OPPORTUNITIES IN THE SCHOOL

We can easily see how these flex time experiences can be valuable to students and their community partners, but what about the impact on teachers and the school itself? What other flextime schedules have been tried?

One high school in NH is the home of an award-winning ELO coordinator, Karen Thompson, who now is the high school's director of K–12 personalized learning. The school board was nationally recognized for its exceptional support of their extended learning program. A take-home point from this high school's long and varied experience with different schedules for ELOs is they have tried different schedules, they have evolved, and they encourage others to give it a try. Just know your ELO and flex time program may evolve too while you find what works best for your school.

This high school originally started their internship program with a seven-class schedule with no flex time. After hearing about the flex time model or FTM time at Brian Pickering's high school and a visit with him, they eventually implemented their intervention program. The intervention program added 40 minutes of flex time to the school schedule. This was helpful to all students, especially ELO students who needed extra time to travel to their community partner sites. Intervention program time was originally 5 days a week but is now 2 days a week.

TIME PROVIDED FOR EXTENDED LEARNING OPPORTUNITY TEACHERS

A high school in NH has four teachers who are designated ELO teachers. They oversee the ELO student's work aided by flex time and an ELO block when they can visit the student at the community partner's business site—usually without needing to hire a sub. ELO teachers teach four core content classes, plus they have a block as an ELO class.

This allows ELO teachers to easily meet with their ELO students in school twice a week to go over the skills and competencies the students are working on, review the reflection journal, and help make sure students are on track to meet their competencies. This also allows for three periods when ELO teachers can go out and meet with ELO business partners. Providing time for teachers to visit the worksite has been very popular with teachers and site supervisors. They both feel more connected to each other and to students' learning.

ELO teachers provide credit for core class credit—be it English, math, science, or other subjects—they just provide it through personalized learning and having students meet core subject competencies via an ELO in a topic in which the student has a particular interest or passion.

One of the key benefits that ELO teachers have seen is that all schools are now measuring student progress in obtaining proficiency in 21st-century skills—the skills that every student will need to succeed in the 21st century. These are skills such as critical thinking, communication, collaboration, and creativity. The ELO teachers mentioned it is easier to show these 21st-century skills with their ELO students. When students are communicating with a community partner on how to meet their learning competencies, while doing a reflection journal and a portfolio describing the process, it is much easier to see those critical skills in use.

ELO students are required to write a reflection piece, to create a resume, and to demonstrate what they have learned in a public exhibition of learning. That exhibition of learning is held once a year during the school day, and every student is either giving an ELO exhibition or going to and listening to an ELO exhibition. Not only is this a rigorous way for students to show their 21st-century skills and the competencies they have acquired at their ELO, but it also generates more interest in ELOs from students who are observing the presentations.

Another impact ELOs have on the school are some of the projects students do. For example, one student doing a biology ELO built a greenhouse at the school. Talk about a lasting legacy and impact on the school! Another student who was working with a math teacher built a school trophy case for the school's many trophies. That ELO included classroom time to learn construction math, pricing, and building the trophy case.

This NH high school's innovative scheduling flexibility includes setting up their advisories with ELO teachers, having many if not all of their ELO students in their advisory. Advisors follow the same students for all 4 years of high school. This helps teachers to get to know and support students even more. ELO students and their advisory teachers meet on Monday and Tuesday when they can work on their 21st-century skills and start planning their Exhibition Day presentation, work on their journal, or just check in to make sure they are on track to meet their competencies.

ELO teachers at this high school mentioned their relationships with ELO students are more developed than with their regular classroom students, especially because of the shared advisory time. Due to flex time, this high school also added a Licensed Nursing Assistant (LNA) class this year that meets twice a week at 2:00 p.m., plus on Saturdays. A unique and wonderful feature is the class is comprised of four NH high school students, plus three adult community members. Applewood Nursing Home pays for each student's course in exchange for at least a 6-month commitment by the students to work at Applewood as an LNA following graduation.

CONCLUSION

So, what kind of students benefit from ELOs? All kinds! From students who struggle academically to class valedictorians, almost all students can learn skills and benefit from a customized ELO. The valuable experiences and mentoring received outside the box, and often outside the traditional school schedule, will likely be a key component in future education models. Think Venn diagram with equal parts experiential learning, online learning, and classroom learning!

The value of ELOs for students, teachers, the school, and the community can be a life-enhancing and sometimes life-changing experience. The importance of having positive business/education connections—made possible by flex time schedules—has increased school/community involvement and has been a source of pride for many school districts. Kudos to schools willing to change their schedules and the ways students earn credit. Kudos as well to site supervisors and community partners who provide such rich learning experiences—and who show students they matter and that what they learn matters—all while showing students the world truly is their classroom.

FINAL CONSIDERATIONS

The most negative aspect of flex time students and teachers mentioned in Bastoni's (2019) study was scheduling. Some students expressed frustration when they could not schedule to a teacher because the teacher was full. This frustration was reported mainly in math and science classes. Another scheduling frustration for students was being scheduled to an activity by a teacher and, consequently, losing the ability to schedule themselves. Although all students expressed an understanding of why this was done (i.e., for their own good or to get a better grade), the majority described this experience as negative and perceived it as a loss of autonomy.

For example, one student in Bastoni's (2019) study said, "I don't really think I had any bad experiences. Except maybe when I really didn't want to do this math project and they [the teacher] signed me up." Another student explained it this way: "Sometimes the teacher will sign you up, and you can't switch out of it, so you're kind of forced to go there, and that does help when they sign you up, but I think it helps and it doesn't." Perhaps this idea can be explained by one of the major connections between the SDT and the flex time model: autonomy. Nine out of twelve students in Bastoni's study reported one of the positive aspects of the flex time model was the ability it provided them to choose the location where they worked.

Reasons for selecting specific locations included comfort with the teacher, liking the physical attributes of the environment (e.g., quiet and fun), being in a space with friends, or valuing the competency of a specific teacher. For example, a student said, "Last year a lot of kids in my chemistry class were struggling, so we would go during [flex time] to another teacher where we would get help." Or, when asked why she continuously booked to a particular classroom, one student explained it this way: "Because it's quiet and you can focus in there. And there aren't a lot of distractions."

In addition to the students' frustrations with scheduling, almost all of the teachers participated in Bastoni's (2019) study also reported some problems with scheduling. At least two teachers reported believing some of their peers (other teachers) did not have students scheduled to them and therefore enjoyed flex time as a second prep. Teachers also mentioned frustration with students being scheduled to their flex time block but not showing up. Many of the teachers believed this was because students were skipping flex time and hanging out in the hallways. Other teachers believed there were too many choices offered to students during flex time, and all of these choices prevented students from accessing the help they might need.

At one particular school, teachers mentioned offering Honors classes during flex time, which created a scheduling challenge (Bastoni, 2019). For example, a teacher said her biggest frustration with flex time was Honors classes for freshmen and sophomores run during this time:

> My biggest pet peeve, though, is certain teachers have been allowed to make it into classes. And, that monopolizes blocks of time that make it so kids can't get the help they need . . . they say it's because Honor's kids don't need help. It's not true. That's not true.

At one school, leadership conducted a survey to better understand how teachers felt about scheduling (Bastoni, 2019). This school asked whether flex time should offer completely heterogeneous classes and then contract with students for Honors classes during flex time, and teachers opinions fell into three categories: those who were against the idea, those who were for the idea, and those who were willing to go either way but wanted more communication and unification on the topic.

Teachers were the largest group to share their opinion on the survey, and they saw using flex time to contract for Honors as a problem. Time, scheduling, and lack of rigor were cited as reasons. One respondent from this group wrote, "I still feel those students would get a better educational experience if they spent more time with similarly academic peers." The second largest respondent group was teachers who believed using flex time to offer Honors was positive.

They listed increased access, increased options for students, scheduling, and the ability to personalize learning as reasons. "I feel very strongly it is a great solution to shrinking options given class size dictates and scheduling conflicts," wrote one respondent. The smallest group included teachers who voiced neutrality or confusion about the topic or asked for clarity, communication, and unification once a decision was reached. For example, one respondent shared, "I believe it is imperative we present a unified front from the teachers and administration on this issue whatever we decide."

Similarly, another respondent from this group of educators wrote, "This is a big issue. I hope we can move forward in a way that is intentional, unified, and puts students first." Some teachers felt offering Honors during this time created more access and saw no issues with it, and others felt it complicated scheduling, overburdened students, and was not a long enough time period. Some students said having Honors during flex time allowed them to take Honors for the first time, of which they were proud, and many advised their peers to use flex time to take Honors.

Administrators from Bastoni's (2019) study mentioned scheduling Honors classes during flex time presents problems and needs to be examined:

> I think [students] also feel it's a little bit stressful because it tries to cram in a whole Honors class into that 40 minutes. For some of those kiddos who are more high anxiety, that is a little more anxiety provoking for them. And I think, for the teachers . . . some teachers feel like it's enough, is what I've heard from them. And other teachers feel as if they need more than just that 40 minutes to provide a true Honors experience. So, it's definitely something we're looking at for next year.

Scheduling Honors classes during flex time can be a contentious issue. Still others said having Honors during this time felt like a lot of work (Bastoni, 2019).

Another significant facet of the flex time model to consider is how the block will be used. Every student interviewed articulated they used flex time to have fun or take a break (Bastoni, 2019). It was also clear they valued the time because doing these two activities was important to them. In fact, nearly every student—and many teachers—mentioned using, or observed students using, flex time as a time to relax.

One student described how she used the time:

> [Flex time] is a good part of the day to really be stress free . . . I feel like it's good because you get to kind of do what you want and if you want to relax, then you can relax.

Another student explained his experience this way: "Most flexible times, I'm usually going to the computer room. I either exploring around on the computers, or just relax, or work on extra work." Describing how teachers fill out the flex time calendar of options, a student said:

> Another teacher might say I'm going to do coloring today or I'm going to do games, something just for them to—usually, this might fall on a Friday—where it's just a relaxing type of mundane activity just to [let students] have a break in the day.

Teachers positively supported students using flex time as a break during the day (Bastoni, 2019). One teacher said:

> I like that it replaces the old-fashioned study hall because kids need a break. When you look at all of the really good private schools they give kids a break. So, if it's good enough for them why isn't it allowed for our awesome public education kids?

Students described flex time as breaking up the "monotony" in the school day or as providing space to "relax." They said break time was "really helpful because if you have a difficult first period you can sign up for where you want to be in [flex time] and de-stress, relax for a minute, catch your breath." Another student said flex time helps because it gives students time to "reorganize their stuff and be stress free for a good period of the day." One teacher explained the time this way:

It gives them a relief valve. So, it probably reduces their stress and anxiety a little bit versus just, "Here's work, go home and work on it." Or versus at my last school, we had traditional study hall where it was basically, sit down and be mostly silent for an hour, and that was hard to manage most of the time.

Interestingly, when asked what recommendations teachers would make to schools interested in implementing the flex time model, the same teacher said the following:

You've got to start off setting down the rules. The kids, they come to you, you take attendance and they stay there. They have to stay there. You have to show them this is a serious work environment. It doesn't mean you're going to force them to do work for you that day if they're coming to just get some work done. But that it's a non-goof-off kind of area.

Break time was not the only way students used flex time in Bastoni's (2019) study. Students mentioned flex time provided them with time to just have fun or to participate in some type of otherwise enjoyable nongraded activity. Many students specifically mentioned movement or creative activities as fun. For example, a student said, "[Flex time has] given me the opportunity to have fun in open gym or signing up for something else I would like to try."

Another student put it this way: "The part I liked most was getting into that drawing class because it was fun." However, the adults we interviewed did mention that flex time gave students the ability to get energy out through movement and praised the time it allowed for students to participate in clubs. For example, when asked to further explain why she participated in fun activities like watching a "short movie," "cup stacking," or "board games," one student said, "It's just good to have fun during school because not everything's fun."

Since research and experience revealed students will, with or without consent, use flex time for fun and breaks, and since many teachers are supportive of these practices, it is recommended schools interested in implementing the flex time model consider giving students the ability to schedule themselves, and a variety of activities should be offered during flex time, including activities that are fun and offer students a break. When it comes to the flex time model, administrators cannot simply make policies or mandates and expect students and teachers will comply, since research reveals many teachers value fun and breaks for students and will support these activities regardless of the administration's stance. Administrators should be careful of how controlling they will be of how the flex time is used. School leaders should keep in mind the tenants of the SDT and make sure they do not devalue autonomy and run the risk of undermining the entire purpose of the flex time model.

It is likely that, in the first year of adopting the flex time model, the staff will recognize elements that are running smoothly and areas that could improve. Adjustments can be made quickly if there is a clear need for change. Most important is for schools to develop a system of feedback that includes teachers and students through surveys and communication systems that allow voices to be heard. What is going well and what could be better are two of the biggest questions to answer.

If there are patterns and consensus of change, then those adjustments can be made. An example of this could be the length of Mentor Mondays. Schools can shorten the length of a Mentor Monday session to allow more time for student supports. This could be during the time in a school year when final projects and assessments may be due.

Administrators can also let their teachers and students be creative by letting them build their own enrichment opportunities. Allowing teachers to grow their opportunities organically and not forced through administrative mandates will likely lead to sustainable success!

Use the Flex Time Survey Questions checklist, given at the end of this book, at the end of each school year with your school's stakeholders to get a good understanding of where all stakeholders are in terms of how the current flex time functions. This practice is ever so valuable to your flex time success, because, as time passes, students' and teachers' needs will inevitably change. The flex time model is built to adapt to your needs. Flexibility allows you to narrow your flex time or expand your flex time offerings and time frames. As a flex time committee, you should not become stagnant.

As an example, after evaluating our first school year with flex time, we saw great improvements from the previous year, but we wanted to provide more specific support—for example, in math, reading, and writing skills—to students who were struggling more in those areas. We also decided to adapt our Mentor Mondays to be more flexible, either with added mentor time or less mentor time, to allow time for different needs at different times. As an example, following a traumatic event, we may have added additional minutes to Mentor Monday or an extra day.

We also decided to take away some mentor time as finals approached at the request of teachers and students, as they were looking for more time for academic support during those times in the school year. Without the survey, we would not have had the information to make these changes to meet the needs that both students and teachers saw as important. This allowed our school to have a stronger flex time model. By doing this after every school year, you can continue to meet the ever-changing needs of students and teachers. This is a recommended best practice for flex time.

Chapter 4

Flex Time Model Checklists
Flex Time Steps to Success

Taking the jump into the flex time world may seem scary, but actually it can be and has been a very smooth process for schools that have taken a few simple steps. We are not saying your school will not run into some bumps early on that need to be addressed and adapted, but it will be worth it. The following steps are a basic guide to provide schools with a structure to help implement flex time into the school day. This is not the only way to go about the process, but it is intended to give you a simple guide in the process, based on information from many schools that have recently implemented flex time into their day. Feel free to take this and be creative in your approach!

1. *Educate your school's staff on flexible schedules*: this can be done in many formats. You could share an article or video on the topic with your staff. This could also be a great topic to discuss in a professional learning community meeting or in other staff meetings. If you have resources to share, including data from this course and other sources, your idea would be taken more seriously. This could even lead to a presentation on flexible schedules during a staff meeting.
2. *Determine staff interest*: after sharing information about flex time with your staff, consider sending out a survey to the staff to assess their level of interest as a whole, and collect any thoughts, questions, or concerns they may have.
    a. A presurvey that would indicate your current schools scheduling strengths and greatest needs can be very helpful because you will likely find that the greatest needs can be solved through flex time.

3. *Build a flex time committee*: if you decide to move forward with building flex time into your school's future schedule, you should build a committee to work on this as a group. This is something you could open up to your staff during a whole school staff meeting. It is important to have an administrator on this team to help put the final process into action.
4. *Create a flex time model to fit your school community*: once you have your committee set up, your group should begin by answering the following questions:
   a. When do you plan on implementing your new flex time schedule? (e.g., next semester or next school year)
   b. What type of flex time schedule will best fit your student's needs?
   c. Will you choose to have a flex time every day, or will you choose to have it on rotating days? There are examples of success with either model.
   d. How long will your school's flex time last? (e.g., 30 minutes, 43 minutes, or 1 hour)
   e. Where will you capture the flex time from your current schedule without lengthening your school day? (e.g., 6 minutes from each block/period, 3 minutes from lunch, and 1 minute from each passing time)
   f. Where will you get funds to pay for the scheduling software? (Administration can help with this process.)
   g. Will students self-schedule or will their teachers schedule them, or a combination of the two? (Enriching Students at enrichingstudents.com can do a demo of both options for you.)
   h. What will your school's flex time teachers' expectations or protocols be? (e.g., teachers cannot overwrite other teachers in the scheduling window)
   i. What flex time options will be available to students? (e.g., extra help, interventions/remediations, extensions, or enrichments social/emotional supports)
   j. Will your school provide credit recovery options during flex time?
   k. Will your school provide ELOs during flex time?
   l. What flex time options will be available to teachers? Will teachers be allowed to hold their Professional Learning Community (PLC) meetings during flextime?
   m. When will your advisory/homeroom/mentor group meet to schedule? How do you plan on organizing these groups? (e.g., eighth-grade survey to group students with a fitting advisor/mentor teacher)

n. Will they be the same group for 4 years of high school? By grade or by alphabet?

5. *Create a finalized schedule to present to school staff*: this staff presentation will allow the whole school to have a voice in the process of finalizing the initial plan for flex time implementation. School buy-in is helpful for any school endeavor to be successful. While it may not be realistic to have 100% of the staff believing in any change, having the majority believing it is the right adjustment for your school will be important to the early success. It is common for even those who doubted the success of flex time to quickly understand its many benefits once you get started.

6. *Make flex time adjustments with the flex time committee based on teacher feedback*: whatever initial decisions you make with your flex time, they do not have to be permanent. Schools are consistently tweaking their model based on what they have learned in the initial implementation. Having a committee and periodic surveys will allow you to make adjustments as you go.

7. *Present the flex time model to your students*: this could be done in a whole school meeting or in small groups. Sharing with them the purpose and vision for your flex time will be important and their questions and feedback should be considered.

8. *Create advisory/mentor groups*: this could be done through a survey to help match students and mentors, by alphabet, by hobbies/interests, by grade, or by any combination of those ideas.

9. *Implement the flex time schedule on the planned implementation date*: the flex time committee should be prepared to meet more frequently during this time to make small adjustments to your school's model based on teacher and student feedback to help the model find positive flow quickly.

10. *Continue to meet as a committee to reevaluate your flex time model and to enhance and grow flex time options for students and staff*: flex time provides endless options for staff and students to be successful.

Administrators should consider letting teachers create their own enrichment ideas when they are ready. Allowing teachers to grow their opportunities organically will likely lead to sustainable success!

FLEX TIME MODEL PROTOCOLS

Once flex time committees in a school complete the build of their schedule to allow for flex time, it is important they create flex time protocols. These protocols are unique to the needs, goals, and priorities of each individual school. These are the expectations that all staff should follow during that time. Some examples of flex time protocols are as follows:

- Teachers can preschedule any students to their room for interventions if they have not met a competency by the end of their course.
- Teachers can't preschedule a student to themselves more than twice per week.
- Schools who use letter grades may say teachers will preschedule students for an intervention if they have grades below D, but teachers do not have to wait this long to preschedule these interventions.
- Teacher prescheduling should take place before 10:00 a.m. on Mentor Mondays or any other predetermined scheduling day when there is no school on a given Monday.
- Prescheduled interventions will always take priority over student scheduling requests.
- Advisors and other academic teachers will not override prescheduled interventions.
- Students who miss a Mentor Monday, or any scheduling day, will be prescheduled to their mentor's room for the remainder of the week and can schedule their classes for the remainder of their week with their mentor upon their return to school.

These are only a few examples of possible protocols your school might follow during this time. It is important to continuously reevaluate your protocols with your school's stakeholders and make appropriate edits when necessary. Some questions your committee may wish to answer in their protocols are as follows:

- How would your school define flex time?
- What are your school's key components of flex time?
- When and how do scheduling days work?
- How does your school define and implement enrichments, extensions, interventions, and supports?

- What are students allowed to do during flex time in your school?
- What are students' expectations during flex time in your school?

SAY FLEX TIME SURVEY QUESTIONS

General School Questions

1. What is the school's current attendance rate?
2. What is the percentage of Ds and Fs or grades below proficiency? By grade and by school?
3. What is your school's current discipline data (number of total incidents) for the school year?

Teacher Questions

1. Teachers please rate our school current flex time to meet the needs of all students in one of the following four categories:
   a. Not effective
   b. Somewhat effective
   c. Effective
   d. Very effective
2. Since the adoption of flex time, students . . .
   a. Turn in less practice or homework
   b. Turn in the same amount of practice or homework
   c. Turn in more practice or homework
3. Since the adoption of flex time the quality of student work is . . .
   a. Not as high quality
   b. The same quality
   c. A higher quality
4. As a teacher, the most valuable use of my flex time is . . . (please rate 1–3)
   a. Assisting students on their work
   b. Assisting students who are most likely not able to stay after school
   c. Tracking my students progress
   d. Meeting with colleagues in a professional learning community
   e. I do not find any value in the use of my flex time

Student Questions

1. As a student, I am able to find time to meet with my teachers when I need help
   a. Always
   b. Sometimes
   c. Never
2. I have time to complete learning experiences personalized to my interests
   a. Always
   b. Sometimes
   c. Never
3. How often do I complete my homework per week?
   a. 1 day
   b. 2 days
   c. 3 days
   d. 4 days
   e. 5 days
4. Have you ever taken advantage of enrichment or extended learning opportunities after school?
   a. Yes
   b. No
5. Have you ever taken advantage of enrichment or extended learning opportunities during school?
   a. Yes
   b. No

Parent Questions

1. Do you feel like your child gets the extra help they need when they need it?
   a. Always
   b. Sometimes
   c. Never
2. Is your child able to stay after school on a consistent basis?
   a. Always
   b. Sometimes
   c. Never

3. What is your child's average grade?
    a. 4.0
    b. 3.5
    c. 3.0
    d. 2.5
    e. 2.0
    f. Below 2.0
4. Does your child feel like they are able to get help from their teachers when they need it?
    a. Always
    b. Sometimes
    c. Never

INTEREST LEVEL FLEX TIME SURVEY FOR TEACHERS

1. Do you feel flex time will be effective in allowing students to turn in more school work?
    a. Not effective
    b. Somewhat effective
    c. Effective
    d. Very effective
2. Do you feel flex time will be effective in allowing students to turn in high quality school work?
    a. Not effective
    b. Somewhat effective
    c. Effective
    d. Very effective
3. Do you feel flex time will enhance your ability to effectively teach your students?
    a. Yes
    b. Maybe
    c. No
    d. Unsure
4. Do you believe flex time will be effective in supporting student academic success and school life balance?
    a. Not effective

b. Somewhat effective
  c. Effective
  d. Very effective

SCHOOL-BASED FLEX TIME SURVEY
ANNUAL QUESTIONS

General School Questions

1. What is the school's current attendance rate?
2. What is the percentage of Ds and Fs or grades below proficiency? By grade and by school?
3. What is your school's discipline data (number of total incidents) after adopting flex time?

Teacher Questions

1. Teachers please rate our school current flex time to meet the needs of all students in one of the following four categories:
   a. Not effective
   b. Somewhat effective
   c. Effective
   d. Very effective
2. Since the adoption of flex time, students . . .
   a. Turn in less practice or homework
   b. Turn in the same amount of practice or homework
   c. Turn in more practice or homework
3. Since the adoption of flex time, the quality of student work is . . .
   a. Not as high quality
   b. The same quality
   c. A higher quality
4. As a teacher, the most valuable use of my flex time is . . . (please rate 1–3)
   a. Assisting students on their work
   b. Assisting students who are most likely not able to stay after school
   c. Tracking my students progress
   d. Meeting with colleagues in a professional learning community
   e. I do not find any value in the use of my flex time

Student Questions

1. As a student, flex time
   a. Has had a negative effect on my learning
   b. Has had no impact on my learning
   c. Has helped me to improve my learning
2. Flex time allows me to personalize my learning by: (rate your top three)
   a. Taking of individualized help
   b. Keeping a better balance between school, activities, and/or work
   c. Taking advantage of extended learning opportunities (e.g., clubs, meetings with counselors, or teacher learning opportunities not connected to my regular class)
   d. Flex time really does not allow me to personalize my learning at all
3. How many flex time sessions does it typically take for you to get caught up when behind?
   a. I really am never behind
   b. One session
   c. Two sessions
   d. Three or more sessions
   e. I am always behind
4. Have you ever taken advantage of enrichment or extended learning opportunities after school?
   a. Yes
   b. No
5. Have you ever taken advantage of enrichment or extended learning opportunity during flex time?
   a. Yes
   b. No

References

Akram, M., Sultan, S., & Ijaz, S. (2014). Students' perceived autonomy support and its impact on achievement goals. *International Journal of Innovation and Scientific Research, 2*(1), 1–7. Retrieved from http://www.ijisr.issr-journals.org/

Anschuetz, N. (2015). Breaking the 4-year myth: Why students are taking longer to graduate. *USA Today.* Retrieved from http://college.usatoday.com/2015/12/16/breaking-the-4-year-myth-why-students-are-taking-longer-to-graduate/

Assor, A., Kaplan, H., & Roth, G. (2002). Choice is good, but relevance is excellent: Autonomy-enhancing and suppressing teacher behaviors predicting students' engagement in schoolwork. *British Journal of Educational Psychology, 72*, 261–278. doi:10.1348/000709902158883

Bastoni, A. (2019). *Examining the connection between self-determination theory and the flexible time model* (Doctoral dissertation). New England College, Henniker, NH.

Brophy, J. (2010). *Motivating students to learn* (3rd ed.). Abingdon-on-Thames, England: Routledge.

Brown, J., & Hall, B. (2016). *SES16: Colchester High School.* Lecture presented at Student Enrichment Summit 2016, Portsmouth, NH.

Caprara, V., Fida, R., Vecchione, M., Bove, G., Vecchio, G., Barbaranelli, C., & Bandura, A. (2008). Longitudinal analysis of the role of perceived self-efficacy for self-regulated learning in academic continuance and achievement. *Journal of Educational Psychology, 100*, 525–534. doi:10.1037/0022-0663.100.3.525

Clarke, J. H. (2013). *Personalized learning: Student-designed pathways to high school graduation.* Thousand Oaks, CA: SAGE.

Cordova, D. I., & Lepper, M. R. (1996). Intrinsic motivation and the process of learning: Beneficial effects of contextualization, personalization, and choice. *Journal of Educational Psychology, 88*, 715–730. doi:10.1037/0022-0663.88.4.715

Cornelius-White, J. (2007). Learner-centered teacher-student relationships are effective: A meta-analysis. *Review of Educational Research, 77,* 113–143. doi:10.3102/003465430298563

Daly-Cano, M., Vaccaro, A., & Newman, B. (2015). College student narratives about learning and using self-advocacy skills. *Journal of Postsecondary Education & Disability, 28,* 213–227. Retrieved from https://files.eric.ed.gov/fulltext/EJ1074673.pdf

Deci, E. L., Hodges, R., Pierson, L., & Tommassone, J. (1992). Autonomy and competence as motivational factors in students with learning disabilities and emotional handicaps. *Journal of Learning Disabilities, 25,* 475–471. doi:10.1177/002221949202500706

Deci, E. L., & Ryan, R. M. (1985). *Intrinsic motivation and self-determination in human behavior.* New York, NY: Plenum.

Deci, E. L., & Ryan, R. M. (1987). The support of autonomy and the control of behavior. *Journal of Personality and Social Psychology, 53,* 1024–1037. doi:10.1037/0022-3514.53.6.1024

Deci, E. L., Ryan, R. M., & Guay, F. (2013). Self-determination theory and actualization of human potential. In D. McInerney, H. Marsh, R. Craven, & F. Guay (Eds.), *Theory driving research: New wave perspectives on self processes and human development* (pp. 109–133). Charlotte, NC: Information Age Press.

Deci, E. L., Ryan, R. M., & Williams, G. C. (1996). Need satisfaction and the self-regulation of learning. *Learning & Individual Differences, 8,* 165–183. doi:10.1016/S1041- 6080(96)90013-8

Deci, E. L., Vallerand, R., Pelletier, L., & Ryan, R. M. (1991). Motivation and education: The self-determination perspective. *Educational Psychologist, 26,* 325–346. doi:10.1207/s15326985ep2603&4_6

Douglas, D. (2004). Self-advocacy: Encouraging students to become partners in differentiation. *Roeper Review, 26,* 223–228. doi:10.1080/02783190409554273

Gabrieli, C., & Goldstein, W. (2008). *Time to learn: How a new school schedule is making smarter kids, happier parents & safer neighborhoods.* San Francisco, CA: Jossey-Bass.

Grolnick, W., & Ryan, M. R. (1987). Autonomy in children's learning: An experimental and individual difference investigation. *Journal of Personality and Social Psychology, 52,* 890–898. doi:10.1037/0022-3514.52.5.890

Hardre, L. P., & Reeve, J. (2003). A motivational model of rural students' intentions to persist in versus drop out of high school. *Journal of Educational Psychology, 95,* 347–356. doi:10.1037/0022-0663.95.2.347

Hattie, J. (2009). *Visible learning for teachers: Maximizing impact on learning.* Oxford, England: Routledge.

Horn, R. A. (2002). *Understanding educational reform.* Santa Barbara, CA: ABC-CLIO.

Hunt, T. C., Carper, J. C., Lasley, T. J., & Raisch, C. D. (2010). *Encyclopedia of educational reform and dissent.* Thousand Oaks, CA: SAGE.

Jack, A. (2018). World class, by Andreas Schleicher: A data driven approach to educational reform. *Financial Times.* Retrieved from https://www.ft.com/

Koestner, R., Ryan, R. M., Bernieri, F., & Holt, K. (1984). Setting limits on children's behavior: The differential effects of controlling vs. informational styles on intrinsic motivation and creativity. *Journal of Personality, 52,* 233–248. doi:10.1111/j.1467-6494.1984.tb00879.x

Kohn, A. (1993). Choices for children: Why and how to let students decide. *Phi Delta Kappa, 75*(1), 8–21. Retrieved from https://journals.sagepub.com/home/pdk

Kohn, A. (2010). How to create nonreaders: Reflections on motivation, learning and sharing power. *English Journal, 100*(1), 16–22. Retrieved from http://www.ncte.org/journals/ej/issues/v100-1

LaMontange, A., & Bernard, M. (2020). School Scheduling Software for Flex Time and RTI. *Enriching Students.* Retrieved from www.enrichingstudents.com/

Malian, I., & Nevin, A. (2002). A review of self-determination literature: Implications for practitioners. *Remedial & Special Education, 23,* 68–74. doi:10.1177/074193250202300202

Malina, R. M. (2002, October 24). Growth, physical activity, and motor development in prepubertal children [Review of the book High altitude: An exploration of human adaption, by T. F. Hornbein & R. B. Schoene]. *American Journal of Human Biology, 14,* 786–795. doi:10.1002/ajhb.10097

National Alliance on Mental Illness. (2017). *Mental health facts: Children and teens.* Retrieved from https://www.nami.org/getattachment/Learn-More/Mental-Health-by-the-Numbers/childrenmhfacts.pdf

National Commission on Excellence in Education. (1983). *A nation at risk.* Retrieved from https://www2.ed.gov/pubs/NatAtRisk/risk.html

Newmann, M. F., & Wehlage, G. G. (1995). *Successful school restructuring: A report to the public and educators.* Washington, DC: American Federation of Teachers.

Pickering, B. A. (2015). *Showcase of model school programs* [Lecture]. Retrieved from https://www.slideshare.net/hczrzavy/neasc-model-showcase20151015

Pickering, B. A., & Bastoni, A. (2016). Flexible blocks enhance personalized learning. *Principal Leadership, 17*(3), 10–12. Retrieved from https://www.nassp.org/news-and-resources/publications/principal-leadership/

Pottage, A. S., & Sillery, M. S. (2016). *The effects of high school flex blocks on students and teachers* (Master's thesis). Retrieved from http://repository.cityu.edu/handle/20.500.11803/32

Reeve, J. (2006). Teachers as facilitators: What autonomy-supportive teachers do and why their students benefit. *The Elementary School Journal, 106*, 225–236. doi:10.1086/501484

Robertson, J. (2010). *Advanced learner perceptions of psychological well-being and school satisfaction into educational settings* (Doctoral dissertation). Retrieved from ProQuest Dissertation and Theses Global database (UMI No. 3438555).

Robinson, K., & Aronica, L. (2015). *Creative schools: The grassroots revolution that's transforming education.* New York, NY: Viking.

Rose, T., & Ogas, O. (2018). *Dark horse.* New York, NY: Harper One.

Rubenstein, L. D. (2011). *Empowering academically underachieving high potential students* (Doctoral dissertation). Retrieved from http://digitalcommons.uconn.edu/dissertations/AAI3468067/

Rubin, R. (2012). Independence, disengagement, and discipline. *Reclaiming Youth Journal, 21*(1), 42–45. Retrieved from http://reclaimingjournal.com/issues-46/

Ryan, R. M., & Grolnick, W. S. (1986). Origins and pawns in the classroom: Self-report and projective assessments of individual differences in children's perceptions. *Journal of Personality and Social Psychology, 50*, 550–558. doi:10.1037/0022-3514.50.3.550

Schleicher, A. (2018). *World class: How to build a 21st century school system.* Paris, France: OECD.

Shernoff, D. J., Csikszentmihalyi, M., Schneider, B., & Steele Shernoff, E. (2003). Student engagement in high school classrooms from the perspective of flow theory. *School Psychology Quarterly, 18*, 158–176. doi:10.1007/978-94-017-9094-9_24

Silva, M., Marques, M., & Teixeira, P. (2014). Testing theory in practice: The example of self-determination theory-based interventions. *The European Health Psychologist, 16*, 171–180. Retrieved from https://www.ehps.net/ehp/index.php/contents/article/view/ehp.v16.i5.p171

Sousa, D. A. (2016). *How the brain learns* (5th ed.). New York, NY: SAGE.

Sousa, D. A. (2017). *Existential psychotherapy: A genetic-phenomenological approach.* New York, NY: Palgrave MacMillan.

Stack, B. (2017, June 5). Flexible periods allow for personalized learning opportunities. *Multi Briefs: Exclusive.* Retrieved from http://exclusive.multibriefs.com/content/flexible-periods-allow-for-personalized-learning-opportunities/education

State of New Hampshire Department of Safety. (2018). *New Hampshire school safety preparedness task force 2018 report.* Retrieved from https://www.governor.nh.gov/documents/school-safety-report-2018.pdf

Toshalis, E., & Nakkula, M. J. (2012). *Motivation, engagement, and student voice.* Boston, MA: Jobs for the Future.

UCLA Center for Mental Health in Schools Program and Policy Analysis. (n.d.). *School engagement, disengagement, learning supports, and school climate.* Retrieved from http://smhp.psych.ucla.edu/pdfdocs/schooleng.pdf

Vygotsky, L. (1978). *Mind in society: The development of higher psychological processes.* Cambridge, MA: Harvard University Press.

Wagner, T., & Dintersmith, T. (2015). *Most likely to succeed: Preparing our for the innovation era.* New York, NY: Scribner.

Wauchope, B. (2009). *Student discipline in New Hampshire schools.* Retrieved from the Carsey Institute website: https://scholars.unh.edu/carsey/86/

Zhao, G. (2014). Art as alterity in education. *Educational Theory, 64,* 245–260. doi:10.1111/edth.12060

About the Authors

Amanda Bastoni, EdD is currently an educational scientist at CAST (www.cast.org). Before working at CAST, Amanda was an accomplished Career and Technical Education (CTE) director and teacher with 20+ years of experience in K–12 educational leadership, journalism, and business. She has a proven record of achievement including being named the 2019 NH CTE Leader of the Year. During her time in education, Amanda has focused on increasing equity and access for special populations in CTE. Specifically, she sought to use the universal design for learning (UDL) to increase pathways for English language learners and females interested in exploring STEM careers.

Amanda helped start innovative cross-disciplinary programs including Robot Algebra, a course that combines math and technology, and Drones in Technology, a course that combines art and technology. Amanda has been selected to sit on numerous education boards including the National Auto Dealers Association Education Board for New Hampshire and through CAST she has lead projects to bring maker spaces to affordable housing developments and map CTE competencies in outdoor recreation across New England. Amanda has written articles for local, regional, and national publications, and in 2020, her first co-authored book was published through Rowman and Littlefield Inc.

Brian Pickering has been involved in education for nearly 35 years. During this time, he has been a teacher, a coach, an athletic director, an assistant principal, a principal, and, most recently, an educational consultant. Over the course of his career, he was named as an NH coach, athletic director, and principal of the year. Pickering served on a variety of leadership committees in education including as a member of the New England Association of School and Colleges.

Pickering received both his bachelor's and master's degrees in education at Keene State College where he also served as an adjunct professor and men's basketball coach. Pickering is also a small business owner and resides in the small village of Drewsville, NH, where he has lived his entire life.

Nathan Bisson is currently the lead school counselor at Fall Mountain Regional High School in NH. He earned his master's degree from Keene State College in 2016. Nathan's passion for helping students succeed and be well has allowed him to share his ideas through multiple professional presentations at venues such as the Inspiring Conversations in Education Conference, Keene State College's Academic Excellence Conference, and at the Council of Public Liberal Arts Colleges (COPLAC) Annual Meeting.

Nathan has had two publications to date. One publication was in the New Hampshire School Counselor Association Newsletter and the other in the spring edition of COPLAC'S *Metamorphosis* research journal. In his free time, Nathan loves spending time with his friends and family as well as playing golf.

www.ingramcontent.com/pod-product-compliance
Lightning Source LLC
Chambersburg PA
CBHW052050300426
44117CB00012B/2065